# Contents

# Introduction

Any introduction to a field of study always has two purposes. The first is to help those starting out in the area to orient themselves and grasp the basic ideas, methods, and writers in the field. The second is to attempt to shape the field of study by drawing attention to certain ways of thinking and by advocating a particular approach over another. While writing this book, I have continually had these two purposes in mind. They represent for me two different audiences. One audience is the general reader. This might be a student taking a course in practical theology, or it might be a practitioner who wants to develop her skills in theological reflection. The other audience is my friends and colleagues who teach practical theology. I want to address these two groups directly in this introduction.

To those exploring practical theology for the first time, I have one or two things to say before we get going. I have tried from the first chapter to present practical theology as something that is already very much part of the life of the Christian community and of the practitioner. Chapter 1 introduces this way of thinking in much more depth, but even if you think you are new to practical theology, you are already an expert in it if you are a part of the Christian community. Just by being a believer and being in the church, you have been introduced to sophisticated and perfectly usable ways of doing practical theology. This doesn't mean you have nothing to learn! The point is that you are not new to this. Also, a field of study like practical theology has a whole host of different writers and thinkers, and as you get into this book you will be introduced to some of these. In several of the chapters I have given samples of the writing and thinking that characterize the academic field of practical theology. My hope is that you will find some of these ideas helpful and exciting and as a result will explore more deeply by reading these books yourself. That said, I understand that some of the things I talk about will not be helpful, and some of the writers I talk about you will almost certainly disagree with. You are not alone. I don't agree with many of the writers I have introduced in this book. They are not here because I think they are right but because they represent ways of thinking that are important—whether you agree with them or not.

In an academic context, the expectation is that we know the whole field and that we are able to present a critical and well-informed argument for the approach we adopt. This is a challenge when starting out in a new area of study, but I have tried to give some guidelines along the way. Of course guidelines are never neutral, including my own, so I want to signal at the start that I have a particular point of view concerning how we should approach practical theology. If you teach practical theology or you are familiar with the field, then you will be interested in and perhaps a little concerned about the approach I take in this introduction. To lay my cards on the table, both for those who are new to the field and for my colleagues in the practical theology world, I will set out what I think is distinctive in this book and how I am attempting to reshape our discipline.

## Reimagining the Clerical Paradigm

In recent years, practical theology has wanted to see itself as not primarily concerned with the training of ministers. Practical theology, it is argued, should move beyond what has been referred to as the "clerical paradigm." I understand the reasons for this and have some sympathy for this view—for instance, where there is a concern to develop a public form of theology that can speak beyond the church. At the same time, there are problems with the wholesale rejection of ministry and the church as a context for practical theology. The key problem with the rejection of the clerical paradigm is that it leaves practical theology without a clear reference point in practice and, indeed, in the life of the church. So while practical theology need not have as its only role the training of clergy, it does need to be fully rooted in the everyday practice of the Christian faith in the church and in the world.

There is, then, a ministerial and a missional dynamic in the way that I have presented the discipline, and this context takes priority in the way that practical theology should be approached. The academic practice of theology is therefore located in relation to the ongoing life of the church. Practical theology is and can be done by those with a wide variety of faith backgrounds—or none. Practical theology done outside the context of a Christian community needs to operate in a very different way than what I have set out in this book. My concern, however, has been to develop a way of doing practical theology that is fundamentally ecclesial and theological in nature, and this introduction assumes a particular relation to commitment and practice.

## Starting with the Everyday and the Ordinary

The orientation of practical theology toward the mission and ministry of the church is both methodological and substantive. It is methodological because the ongoing life of the church is itself practical theology. Christian believers and ministers come to the discipline already formed as skilled and highly able practical theologians. Students and others who study the discipline, simply by being part of the ongoing life of the church, have absorbed and participated in sophisticated and effective ways of doing practical theology before they walk into the classroom or even before they pick up this book.

Practical theology, therefore, must start by first encouraging students to recognize how they already exercise their ministry and Christian lives by making use of practical theology in their everyday lives. This everyday or ordinary practical theology is not replaced by formal study, but it is enhanced by it. Practical theology must therefore set out to build on, rather than primarily seek to critique, ways of thinking and operating that are common in church contexts. This requires the practical theologian to have close engagement and empathy with churches of all kinds and with the ways individuals in these churches habitually think theologically.

## Reembracing Applied Theology

Practical theologians have for some time now presented the discipline as quite distinct from forms of theology that are applied, where "applied" refers to kinds of theology that work from doctrinal or biblical thinking toward the practice of the church. Practical theology, it is argued, reverses this process by starting from practice and experience and then moving toward theological formulation. This positioning of practical theology is problematic and mistaken for three reasons. First, in the everyday life of the church, most reflection on practice takes place through a deep engagement with the Scriptures. Christian communities have historically renewed themselves, critiqued their practice, and generated ways of witness in the world by reflecting on the Bible in sermons, Bible studies, and personal study. It is simply counterintuitive (and flies in the face of proven experience) to confront students in the classroom with a discipline that says you can only reflect properly when you start with practice.

The second reason I think the rejection of applied theology is mistaken is more technical and academic. Starting points are methodologically problematic. So, for instance, even if we say that we must start by reflecting on experience, the truth is that we have each been shaped already by a community context. This means that we carry into the reflection on experience a theologically shaped perspective. The same observation holds true in relation to what we have called applied theology. So while it may appear that we are starting with the Scriptures, in fact we bring our experience of life and of the church to the Scriptures. Doctrine or experience cannot ever be bracketed out of the equation because we each carry them together within ourselves. The experience of the Christian community and the doctrine of the community are in us and have formed us. This is what I have called the "affective gravitational pull of the Church."[1] "Affective" refers to the feelings and emotions the church imparts to us. These act as a force in our lives. The gravitational pull of the church is both doctrinal and experiential, and practical theology needs to accept that methods set out in the classroom and in the pages of an academic text are never as clean or straightforward when they are used by people in the context of the church. The affective gravitational pull means that starting points become inevitably blurred.

The third reason I think the rejection of applied theology is a mistake is that the turn to experience as a starting point for theology is a political move that puts practical theology firmly on the liberal side of the debates in modern theology. I will explore this in more depth in the next section.

1. Ward, "Blueprint Ecclesiology."

## Moving beyond Liberal Theology

Modern theology has a basic fault line running through it between liberal theology, which prioritizes experience over doctrine, and conservative theology, which prioritizes doctrine over experience. Both the rejection of applied forms of theology and the uncritical acceptance of practical theology as distinct because it starts with practice are problematic because these views situate the discipline solely within the liberal tradition. This is a problem not because I would advocate an uncritical conservative approach. Rather, I argue for a collapse of these two distinctions—the liberal and the conservative—into one another. The distinction is therefore artificial.

Arguing that the discipline of practical theology starts from experience is problematic because it prejudges the conversation and effectively outlaws important and constructive theological resources and voices on an ideological basis. I am not objecting here to a critical choice of sources in doing theology, nor am I rejecting liberal theological approaches per se. My point is not so much that this position is argued for in practical theology as that it is asserted as the very basis for the discipline; as such, liberal theology is imposed by force or inserted into the minds of students by stealth. I think students need to be introduced to a range of approaches and methods, and then they should be allowed to make up their own minds. Doctrinal ways of doing practical theology need to be considered alongside those that start from experience, and both should be regarded as possible ways of approaching the discipline.

## Expanding the Canon of Practical Theology

In this book I adopt a broad understanding of practical theology. I define practical theology as any way of thinking that takes both practice and theology seriously. This is not really a definition; rather, it is a decision to include within the accepted academic work in practical theology a whole range of material that might not normally be seen as belonging to the discipline. This is again an attempt to reverse the tendency whereby practical theology limits itself to those who have been part of the academic guild. This concentration has come about because practical theologians have felt for some time that they are marginalized in the academy. This has led them to seek to bolster the position of their discipline by creating a convention that rewards and supports a way of working that continually refers to the key figures within the discipline. This orientation toward a particular canon has been reinforced by academic conferences and journals intended to build the discipline.

I am very much in sympathy with these developments within the discipline. The problem, however, is that even as practical theology has grown, a range of moves toward practice and culture have been made within the wider theological world. I say more about these developments later in the book, but the key insight here is that some of the most exciting and innovative work in practical theology might not actually be done by people who call themselves practical theologians. There is, then, a much larger conversation across the theological world that the academic discipline of practical theology needs to acknowledge and place itself within.

## Developing a Theology of Practical Theology

It might seem odd, but I am not sure that practical theologians have spent terribly much time developing a theology of the discipline. One of the reasons sometimes given for this is that starting from experience to some extent precludes a theological prolegomena. But this is actually not the case, because the decision to start from experience, as I have just pointed out, is itself a theological move. So a deep and pervasive theology underlies most practical theology, but it is not usually made explicit. Because it is largely implicit, there is a tendency for this theology to be assumed rather than set out as a position. To avoid falling into the same trap in this book, I have set out a theology of practical theology. My starting point has been to explore the nature of theology as the knowledge of God. I argue that knowledge of God is distinct from other kinds of knowledge because God cannot be known in the same way that we know about other things. Knowing God is participatory in nature. In other words, the practice of theology is sharing in the life of God.

## Encountering God in Prayer and Worship

The theological approach to practical theology that I advocate assumes a relational engagement with God as the basis for knowing. Specifically, I see practical theology as situated in an ongoing and regular encounter with

God through prayer and worship. These practices are not simply the field for research and study; they are also the very basis on which that study is made possible. The reason for this is my understanding of practical theology as a discipline that takes both practice and theology seriously. Taking theology seriously means fostering a continual relationship with God. Worship and prayer is the basis for practical theology because it enables a theology that is relational and that starts with encounter and wonder. Worship, then, is not simply affirmation of belief; it is the encounter with what is beyond theological expression. Worship engenders a knowing and not knowing that develops humility as well as a confidence in the practice of theology.

# 1

# Practical Theology as the Ordinary Life of the Church

"So what kind of theologian are you?" asked the US immigration officer with my passport in his hand.

"A practical theologian," I said.

"I didn't think any theology was practical," he replied.

I was not sure if this had to do strictly with security, but I spoke my mind. "I like to think that all theology can be practical."

He smiled in a way that seemed to imply I was clearly deluded, and he let me into the country.

Whatever the immigration officer thought, there is such a thing as practical theology—with its own distinctive theories, methods, and literature. This book is a guide to this field. In the 1950s one of the key figures in the contemporary development of practical theology in the United States, Seward Hiltner, talked about a "pastoral perspective" in theology. What he meant was that there was a way of seeing that came from pastoral practice.[1] The pastoral perspective, he argued, gives a distinctive shape to theological study. So while there are the traditional theological disciplines of biblical studies, church history, Christian ethics, and systematic theology, there

---

1. Hiltner, *Preface to Pastoral Theology*. Hiltner said there were other perspectives that come from the practice of the church, but his main focus was on pastoral ministry.

is also a way of doing theology that arises from and seeks to inform the pastoral practice of the church. Those who adopt this pastoral perspective do biblical studies and systematic theology and so on, but they do them in a distinctive way. They foreground the questions and issues that come out of their ministry. So the pastoral perspective involves a kind of theology that tries to critique and inform the pastoral practice of the church.

In more recent times, there has been a tendency to downplay the link to pastoral ministry. Practical theology, it has been argued, should never be the sole preserve of clergy, but Hiltner's suggestion that there is a pastoral perspective makes a great deal of sense. This perspective is not limited to professional clergy or to pastoral ministry; it is much broader than that. It is a perspective that comes from the practice of faith in all its forms and with all its questions and challenges.

## Theology and Practice

Saying that all theology can be pastorally oriented or practical is one thing; working through what this actually means is another thing entirely. It is, for instance, quite possible to turn this assertion on its head and say that Christian practice itself is inherently and profoundly theological. If theology can be practical, then practice is also theological. Practical theology is situated in this web of interrelated possibilities and issues. The truth is that the word "theology" itself is complex. When we try to combine theology with practice, things become even more complicated. Complexity is not necessarily a problem to be solved; it is just the way things are. Rowan Williams says that the theologian always starts "in the middle of things."[2] Being in the middle means that there is no defined starting point or clear methodology for theology. We are simply where we are. Most significantly, every believer is situated in the life, thought, and practices of a community. Theologians learn to think about God by sharing in a communal conversation that characterizes church. So while practical theology may be complex and at times hard to pin down, a clue to making any sense of it lies in what it means to be in the middle of the Christian community.

American practical theologian Bonnie Miller-McLemore identifies four uses of the term practical theology. Practical theology, she says, is an aca-

2. Rowan Williams, *On Christian Theology*, xii.

demic discipline among scholars, and it is an activity of faith undertaken by believers. Practical theology is also a method for thinking and a subject area in a curriculum. These different "enterprises," as she calls them, are distinct. They have different audiences and ways of operating, but they are also interconnected. So while practical theology refers to the activity in the church in which believers "sustain a life of reflective faith in the everyday," it is also a specific method or a way of understanding theology in practice.[3] This method shapes the way that practical theology is taught as part of the curriculum in theological education.

Each of these ways of understanding practical theology suggests a different location, from congregation and community to daily life, and from the library to fieldwork and the classroom. These four understandings, says Miller-McLemore, are not to be seen as mutually exclusive. They are connected and interdependent. Together they show the range and complexity of practical theology. "Practical theology is multivalent. It appears in a broad array of spaces and places." Yet although it is clearly a discipline within the academy with related methods and curriculum, the ultimate purpose of practical theology, she says, lies in the pursuit of an "embodied Christian faith."[4] Practical theology in its different shapes and forms finds its basic orientation in the life of the church. It is never an end in itself. So while it may have the usual kinds of academic expectations and ways of working, it is always operating in relation to the ongoing life of the Christian community. Practical theology has an ecclesial perspective and purpose.

Rowan Williams's sense that theology always starts "in the middle" supports the idea that church is a key starting point for practical theology. Theological thought, he suggests, operates in three different ways: celebration, communication, and critique. Theology begins as celebration. To celebrate, says Williams, is to make use of language to express, in the deepest and most profound way, the richness of God. Celebration is seen in liturgy, in hymn writing, and in preaching, but it is also present in theological writing. Celebration is seen in the writing of Dante or the poetry of the fourteenth-century English peasant William Langland. It is in conventions of Byzantine iconography, and it can also be seen in some

3. Miller-McLemore, *Companion to Practical Theology*, 5.
4. Ibid.

contemporary worship songs.[5] Orthodox theology, says Williams, operates primarily as celebration.

Celebration, however, has a tendency to become locked in its own expression. So while there is a rigor and discipline to this work, theology as celebration can become absorbed or frozen in the cross-referencing of symbols and images. When this happens, there is a need for talk of God that attempts to persuade and commend. This is theology as communication.

Communicative theology attempts to "witness to the gospel's capacity for being at home in more than one cultural environment." It is a theology that sets out to show how this gospel can emerge from a sustained engagement with complex areas of thought with confidence. Communicative theology can be seen throughout Christian history. It is there in the work of the apologists Clement and Origen as they sought to "colonize" Stoic and Platonic philosophy with the Christian faith. It is there in the early English poetry of the "Dream of the Rood," which connects a theology of the cross to Germanic themes of the hero, and it is there in more recent times in the work of liberation theologians. Communicative theology, for Williams, "involves a considerable act of trust in the theological tradition, a confidence that the fundamental categories of belief are robust enough to survive the drastic experience of immersion in other ways of constructing and construing the world."[6]

Complexity and clarity have their respective problems. Communication can oversimplify or get lost in the terms and frameworks that have been borrowed from the surrounding culture. Celebration can become a closed and self-congratulatory system. Critical theology operates as a corrective to these tendencies. In the early church, Williams says, alongside the generation of doctrine was the apophatic tradition, also known as negative theology, which is an approach to theology that emphasizes the mystery of God. Negative theology, says Williams, plays a significant role simply by offering a warning note alongside the elaboration of doctrine.[7] Theology in a critical mode can be either conservative or liberal. It can advocate a reevaluation of doctrine or the abandonment of long-held positions. Critical theology is not necessarily an end in itself; its purpose is, for instance, to generate a better or more nuanced kind of celebratory theological expression.

5. Rowan Williams, *On Christian Theology*, xiii.
6. Ibid., xiv.
7. Ibid., xv.

The suggestion that practical theology is evident in the life of the church as celebration, communication, and critique is significant. It introduces the idea that practical theology can be detected and undertaken in a wide range of expressions. So for instance, communicative theology might be seen in sermons and doctrines but is also evident in academic writing, hymn writing, and theater. Celebratory theology is evident in the visual arts, poetry, abstract theological writing, and many other places. Critical theology similarly exists in academic writing, but it can also be found in spiritual practices and contemplative prayer. So Williams does not limit theology to an academic discipline alone but sees it as part of the everyday conversation and communal life of the church.[8]

Williams's understanding of theology offers a nuanced and creative new perspective on practical theology. It expands Miller-McLemore's idea that practical theology exists as four enterprises. So the practical theology that can be seen in the ongoing life of the church might be at times celebration or communication, but it can also be critique. The methods that characterize practical theology might, in turn, be expanded to make room for the ways in which poets, artists, and hymn writers construct visions of God. Practical theology should never be reduced to a topic for an assignment or a thesis for examination. The academic curriculum needs to start by exploring how believers are already and always practical theologians because they are in the "middle." So, while there is a discipline that we call practical theology, with teachers, conferences, and academic journals, these only make sense as they are seen in relation to the church. This basically is Hiltner's point. There is a perspective that comes from being engaged in the life of the church. This perspective for Hiltner is "pastoral"; we might add "missional" or "political," but the point is that these are derived from a location within the Christian community. This is what makes practical theology *practical*, and, more crucially, it is what makes practical theology *theological*.

## Practical Theology in the Life of the Church

Most people, even if they have been part of the church for some time, have never heard that there is such a thing as practical theology. So the

8. Ibid.

first encounter they have with the term comes when they sign up for some kind of theological study. This experience of practical theology as part of formal theological education actually gives a false impression because, as we have been exploring, Christians are already practical theologians simply because they are "in the middle" of the celebration, communication, and critical conversation that are characteristic of the Christian community. Church life makes each of us into wise, skilled, and highly accomplished theologians. This is what American practical theologian Craig Dykstra calls "ecclesial imagination."[9] Communities and individuals, says Dykstra, have a wisdom that comes from a shared life and history. This wisdom means that before they ever encounter the academic discipline of practical theology, believers are theologians.

At its heart, there is something ordinary and everyday about practical theology. One of the leading practical theologians in the United Kingdom, Jeff Astley, speaks about the "ordinary theology" of believers.[10] From the writing of Bonnie Miller-McLemore and Rowan Williams it is clear that theology operates as a natural and everyday part of the life of the Christian community. Theology at the level of practice is "ordinary." It is the basic way of speaking and living in the Christian community. Being a part of a church inevitably means that we share in an ongoing conversation about God. By being a disciple, believers are always engaged in trying to make sense of what it means to live the Christian life. So just by being active in the life of the church and by seeking to express a faithful Christian life in communities and the wider society, Christians are doing practical theology. There are a number of practices that can be used to further explore ordinary practical theology in the everyday life of the church. In the next section we examine five of these practices: remembering, absorbing, noticing, selecting/editing, and expressing.

### Remembering

Week in and week out, through Bible reading, preaching, singing, praying, and celebrating the Eucharist, Christians remember. Remembering expresses how the church is shaped and formed by the gospel. In worship, the doctrinal and biblical ways of speaking are embodied and lifted up in

9. Dykstra, "Pastoral and Ecclesial Imagination," 41.
10. Astley, *Ordinary Theology*, 62–63.

performance. Worship is a practical theology, but it challenges any clear divide between practice and theology. A good example of this is the way that many churches sing contemporary worship songs. The lyrics of a particular song may be what Williams calls a "celebratory theology"; in other words, they may be a profound and moving expression of the being of God. They may also be a deliberately communicative kind of theologizing designed to convict and convince.

John Wesley, for instance, saw his hymns as a means to teach the faith. Yet what are obviously doctrinal or theological expressions in song lyrics are transformed in the act of singing. Singing animates and brings doctrine alive. It is not simply that music connects theological ideas to emotions. Something physical happens as we sing. We draw the words into ourselves and we form them with our own bodies. We feel them vibrating in the air as they are made sound by the bodies around us.

Songs and singing build communities in mysterious ways. Community itself exists as a cohabitation with those in the church, but we are also indwelt by the presence of God. Singing celebrates and enacts community. As the community sings, it remembers, and as it remembers, Jesus becomes present by the power of the Spirit. Singing as a form of remembering, therefore, is more than simply a cognitive recollection.

Singing is one of many forms of ordinary practical theology. Australian practical theologian Terry Veling says that theology only becomes comprehensible when we see it as something that indwells practice. "As the Christian community engages in the practices of prayer, study, hospitality, forgiveness," says Veling, "we begin to deepen our understanding of what the kingdom of God is all about, and what it means to be a people of God."[11] Veling is talking about the ways in which communities collectively and individually engage in practices of remembering. Remembering is fundamentally about the gospel story. Through prayer, singing, and other kinds of practice, Christians do not simply recall what has happened in the past. The story rises up, envelops us, and takes us into itself. The presence of Christ through the Spirit lifts us and carries us in the story. As this happens, the believer is opened up to the future, transformed by the hope of the kingdom. This kind of practical theology is fundamental and basic to the life of the church. In fact, without it there would be no church at all.

11. Veling, *Practical Theology*, 4.

### Absorbing

One of the most influential figures in practical theology, Don Browning, describes the practice of the church as being "theory laden." "By using the phrase *theory-laden*," he says, "I mean to rule out in advance the widely held assumption that theory is distinct from practice. All our practices, even our religious practices, have theories behind and within them."[12] In other words, church life is filled with ideas about God. These ideas, or theories, are embedded in communal practice. Church practice is theological not just in the things that are said but also in the way communities share in the life of God. Eating meals together is theological, sitting in pews is theological, interacting on Facebook is theological. The life of every congregation is distinctively influenced and shaped by particular ways of understanding and seeking to express a theological vision. Churches are theology laden. So just by being part of a community, we start to share in the rich theological story of the church.

Churches are laden with different kinds of theory and different kinds of practice. These differences make up distinctive traditions within church life. By being part of a community, we internalize and absorb these particular ways of being Christian. So we might start to identify ourselves as Baptist, Pentecostal, Catholic, Lutheran, or Anglican. Alongside formal denominational kinds of identity are ways that Christians understand themselves that are more specific. These might include labels such as liberal, charismatic, orthodox, progressive, or conservative. It is not at all unusual for Christians to have a very close identification with a particular tradition. These kinds of identification—and we all carry them with us to some extent—are evidence of the ways in which, through sharing in communal life, believers start to absorb theological perspectives. Our sense of who we are as Christians comes out of what we have absorbed. We are, as Williams says, theologians who start by being "in the middle of things."[13]

Absorbed theology is theology that has made the shift from something that is external and expressed by others to something that is part of us. So just as we see the life of the church to be theory laden, so we see our own lives as Christians in a similar way. Practical theologian Edward

---

12. Browning, *Fundamental Practical Theology*, 6.
13. Rowan Williams, *On Christian Theology*, xii.

Farley talks about the ways in which theology becomes a virtue or a habituated part of the believer. He uses a term for this that originates with Aristotle: "habitus." In medieval times, says Farley, theology was understood as something that became a habitus, a knowledge that became a habit, "an enduring orientation and dexterity of the soul, . . . a cognitive disposition and orientation of the soul, a knowledge of God and what God reveals."[14]

The idea of habitus focuses our attention on the extent to which "theology" is inherently practical. We absorb the knowledge of God, and in turn we find ourselves absorbed into the life of God. We take in theology through our participation in the life of the Christian community, through fellowship, preaching, missional action in the world, singing songs, and the sacraments; as we do so, this sharing takes us up into the life of God. Absorbed theology in this sense is the most basic and ordinary form of practical theology. We live out of our absorbed theology. Practical theology in all of its manifestations starts from this residue within us that has been shaped by the life of the Christian community.

### Noticing

The habitus of faith not only shapes practice; it also influences the way believers view the world. Through prayer, Bible reading, worship, and fellowship, Christians develop ways of seeing. A good example of this is intercessory prayer. Intercession is often very personal. Many Christians have prayer lists that act as a reminder to pray regularly for those who are sick or who have particular problems. Believers may differ on how exactly they see the Spirit working or God's grace having an effect, but this kind of prayer is an everyday and ordinary part of the Christian life. Prayer is an enacted practical theology. In many churches, prayers for healing form a regular part of worship. This can be an extension of the Eucharistic practice of "going up to communion," or in more charismatic churches, services may end with a time in which people are prayed for by a designated ministry team. These kinds of prayer ministries embody an ordinary form of theology. They perform and make present the practical theology of a God who sees and, above all, cares. Praying for others becomes a way of noticing suffering and hardship.

14. Farley, *Theologia*, 35.

In public worship, intercession combines the personal and the political. Churches habitually pray for the world. We call to mind the images we have seen on the television screen and place them at the feet of God. We struggle to make sense of the senseless, the tragic, and the downright evil. Praying for the world is a corrective to the current emphasis on spiritual experience and "getting the most out of church." Intercessory prayer acts as a moral compass in Christian liturgy. Praying for those who are in need and for the world in which we live develops habits of seeing. These habits, because they are formed through prayer, are infused with the gospel. In this way, noticing becomes a practical theology that is at the same time a spiritual practice. Noticing and praying, of course, often lead to action. Christians give money and time to charity; they are active in volunteering and in campaigning. All of these practices arise from noticing. Seeing comes from a place "in the middle"—in the middle of the Christian community, in the middle of society, and in the middle of the gospel story.

### Selecting/Editing

The Christian life is made up of a range of habits and practices that involve making choices. A good example is listening to a sermon. Listening is not just passive. When we listen, we pick up on things said that are of particular interest or relevance to us. At the same time, we also let some of the things said pass us by. We select as we make meaning out of a sermon. Of course it is not just those in the pews who have selected. The preacher has also made choices in writing the sermon. It is not possible, or indeed advisable, to try to say everything about a passage. The preacher has to focus on what she feels God is saying through the readings. She has made a choice between different possible messages. Selecting what to say or not say is one of the most basic kinds of ordinary practical theology.

Selecting doesn't simply involve us in the details of preaching or the content of a sermon. We make choices that are much larger. If we move to a new town, for instance, we have to choose which church we want to attend. This involves selecting between different options. Then there are all the choices that make up life: what career we might follow, how we are going to bring up the kids, how we should spend our retirement, which charities we should support, and so on. Everyone makes choices in life, and Christians generally try to make choices that are shaped by their faith. Making

Christian choices is a complex matter. We might spend quite some time praying, reading the Bible, and talking with friends when we have to make a particularly significant choice. We might even seek out more specialized help in counseling or through reading Christian books. Some people go to events and conferences looking for help in selecting the "right" thing for them. This kind of selecting is a form of critical practical theology.

Closely related to selecting is the practice of editing. There was a time when editing was limited to professionals in the publishing business. So for instance, as new hymnbooks came out, editors were accustomed to updating the lyrics. Verses that were seen as obscure were left out. In our contemporary context, hymns that use overtly male terms are sometimes changed to be more inclusive. With the digitization of songs and hymns, we are now able to do this kind of editing at a much more local level. We can remove lines, write new verses, and change things around as we see fit. In Christian worship more generally, this ability to manipulate and edit prayers and liturgies has become an everyday occurrence. Gone are the days when there was one set prayer book. Ministers have become accustomed to constructing services from a range of different sources available online. Actually, even where services are formally written down in prayer books, ministers have often edited or given things their own particular style. In Pentecostal and charismatic churches, where the liturgy is more informal, worship leaders also act as editors as they make decisions about what song to sing or as they decide to repeat sections in a song or even improvise their own lyrics as the Spirit moves them. So in different ways, Christians are familiar with the notion of editing.

Fundamental to editing is a sense that things can be done differently. To edit, you need not only a familiarity with the particular source, whether songs or liturgical texts, but also the ability to envision something new. Editors, out of habit, recognize that the way it has been so far expressed or the order in which things have been done in the past might be changed and made not just different but better. This too is a kind of theological reflection. Ministers and those involved in leading worship regularly look for ways to learn more and find different perspectives on their practice. There are a great many training courses and conferences on Christian worship as well as web-based resources and magazines. It is likely that very few of these resources identify themselves as practical theology, but that is what they are.

### Expressing

Practical theology as expression includes not only all occasions where Christians talk about faith but also the many ways in which faith is lived. Living the life of faith is often called discipleship, an active following of Christ in the everyday. Being a disciple is complex. It involves business ethics and family life, political commitments and lifestyle choices. Christians differ on what precisely it means to be a disciple. Some, for instance, advocate pacifism, and others serve in the armed forces.

The bottom line, however, is that in seeking to be a follower of Christ, every Christian is *expressing* faith. This is a lived and everyday form of practical theology. It involves choices based on an understanding of the gospel and creative ways of operating in the complex and confusing fields of economic, political, and personal life. One way the idea that life is an expression of the gospel has been talked about is through the concept of witness. Witness encapsulates the notion that Christians are called to express their faith in and through their lives. Witness therefore combines the gospel and the embodied, but it is also relational. There are those to whom believers are called to witness. Expression therefore has two reference points. To be a witness, it is necessary to be faithful to Christ, but there is also a calling to communicate in particular places and particular times.

Rowan Williams makes it clear that theological expression takes place in a variety of forms and genres. Expression is not limited to the sermon or the theological treatise. In the everyday life of the church, there are actually a great many ways in which individuals and groups express faith. An example of this is the different ways we talk about the word "church." Church in common parlance means a building. You go to church or get married in church. But church also refers to the communal life of a congregation. So we hear people saying how much they enjoy being part of the local church or how much they will miss their church when they have to move away. Here it is not so much the building that is being talked about but the fellowship of believers who meet in that place.

Both church as building and church as community are expressions. They are an everyday and material form of practical theology. Church buildings have a theological language or symbolic code woven into the fabric. Different kinds of churches are different kinds of theological expression, from great cathedrals to small chapels. Yet networks of friendship and care are, in their way, also expressions of faith. In church buildings we see the expression of architects and artists of all kinds. From stained glass windows to plain white walls, faith has an aesthetic and a sensibility in the physical.

Communities likewise express faith in different ways. Some are highly active in campaigning for justice and politics; others hold rather quiet meetings over coffee and cake. Each expresses a practical theology, an interpretation of what faith means as it is lived out in community.

## Reasons to Do Practical Theology

There are all kinds of ways in which the ordinary life of the church involves people doing practical theology. Alongside the everyday kinds of theologizing are times when individuals, groups, and congregations feel the need to take up the challenge of more focused theological reflection. A study group, for instance, may become a place for the kind of critical theology that Rowan Williams envisages. Conferences on leadership or worship are common in some areas of the church, and these too may help generate a kind of practical theology that offers a constructive critique of the life of the church. As well as these kinds of events, there are more structured training courses and degree programs run by seminaries and universities.

While formal education in practical theology may introduce new ways of thinking or new perspectives, it is important to realize that what happens in the classroom and the seminary grows out of and feeds into the everyday life of the Christian community. This connection to the church is not simply a theory. Students, whether they are training for ministry, working in Christian charities, or members of congregations, bring the church with them. Students are "in the middle." They are shaped by their communities, and being in the middle means they want to study precisely because of the questions and issues that come out of the everyday practice of faith.

So there are a number of reasons people want to take part in theological study. At the most basic level, there is often simply a desire to learn. It is natural that if faith means a great deal to us, we want to know more. Knowing more does not inevitably take us to practical theology. It is possible to study the history of the church, for instance, apart from any specific faith commitments, but no study is ever free of interpretative perspectives. Even the decision to try to be objective is itself a kind of bias.

Studying church history is always in some way or another a conversation about ourselves. We dig deeper into our roots, we examine where we have come from, and we research how we have got to where we are. Studying the history of the church in this way is not very far from Hiltner's idea of a pastoral perspective. Knowing more becomes a part of the processes of theological reflection. It helps Christians think deeply about our present situation, and it gives us ways to critique and inform what we are doing as individuals and as Christian communities. What is true for church history is also the case for theology. The desire to know more about the Bible, for instance, often comes out of a sense that this kind of study will make a difference to how believers live their lives. In an academic context, biblical studies does not generally make questions of application and relevance a focus for study. Nevertheless, these kinds of motivations often lie beneath the surface, and hidden and sometimes unspoken assumptions find their way into academic study. Practical theology takes these unspoken motivations and brings them into the heart of the conversation. Valuing practice means that the practical theologian is drawn toward the transformative significance of theological thought. This kind of theological reflection engages with disciplines such as church history and biblical studies, but it does so through the lens of practice.

The desire to know more often comes out of a realization that we do not know enough. It is not at all unusual for practice to get ahead of theory. This could be a simple situation—for instance, being asked to lead a group study on a particular issue. It is more than likely that we will need to prepare in some way to lead this kind of group. Preparation might involve an online search and visiting a few websites. We might read magazine articles or books. In structured courses, we may be expected to use specially written materials. Here again, it is highly probable that none of these resources will identify themselves as practical theology, but the mere fact that they are being used to help a group think about the Christian faith transforms them into practical theology. It is not the specific material but the process of application that constitutes theological reflection.

Not knowing enough occasionally becomes an urgent matter. In a pastoral situation, it might suddenly become essential to learn more about a particular issue such as drug addiction or eating disorders. For those new to pastoral ministry or leadership in the church, such crises can be quite common. But even those who are very experienced and have professional training occasionally have a sense that they do not know enough. This sense of a gap in knowledge can become particularly acute when someone, for example, has trained as a community activist or as a youth worker and his or her practice seems to have developed in ways that no longer fit with previous theological understanding. This experience is actually common, and it is one of the main reasons ministers and others who are professionally engaged in different kinds of ministry want to return to academic institutions to study theology, and practical theology in particular.

Practitioners often find that they have lost their theological bearings. Losing a theological orientation is not quite the same as losing faith. The normal pattern is that practitioners continue to find their personal faith to be meaningful and helpful, and God is still a reality in their lives. At the same time, they start to become more and more hazy about how this personal faith connects to what they do. A good example of this is the person who trains as a counselor. Suddenly they are introduced to a whole range of ways of helping people. Many of the theories that inform the practice of counseling have little or no explicit connection to Christian theology as it is discussed in church. At first the belief that caring for people is a Christian calling may be enough, but over time many practitioners start to experience unease with where they find themselves. It is like taking an inflatable raft out onto the water. Drifting with the current seems pleasant, but after a while you can find yourself quite far from where you are meant to be. Practical theology is one of the ways that practitioners can look up from where their professional ministry has taken them and find ways to reorient themselves. This might take the form of finding new ways to think about God and the practice of ministry, or it may simply mean finding ways to connect absorbed theology and the tradition of the church to new forms of practice and professional life.

Losing our theological bearings is actually a normal Christian experience. Most renewal movements in the church come out of a sense that previous theologies are not adequate. Often this sense of theological dislocation comes from cultural change. In recent years, for instance, there has been a vigorous debate about the future shape of the church. Some people have argued that because of changes in popular culture and in society more generally, there is a missiological imperative to develop new ways of being church. Previous patterns of ecclesial life, it is suggested, are locked into older social forms. Changes in the way people relate to their neighborhood, digital technologies, and shifting patterns within the family all seem to indicate that traditional churches based on the parishes or the congregation may need to adapt in significant ways.

Another example of changes that seem to require us to rethink how we practice faith is the experience of globalization. The exposure to 24/7 live news brings the multicultural and religiously pluralistic nature of the world into our living rooms. At the same time, mass migration means that most of us live in communities that are many times more diverse than our parents ever experienced. With a much more developed awareness of the different kinds of faith comes the need to reexamine previous certainties. At the same time, there are changes in society such as the various debates that surround human sexuality and developments in genetics.

These kinds of changes raise theological questions that absorbed or habituated theologies may not be immediately able to answer. At the same time, there is a sense that theology should be able to help us find ways to practice faith in these changing contexts. For those who are confronted with these kinds of issues, practical theology offers a way to look for reorientation and new ways of thinking.

## The Purpose of Practical Theology

As my experience with the US immigration officer illustrated, it is a popular misconception that theology has no practical purpose. There is, however, a recognizable truth expressed by that kind of sentiment. Academic forms of theology tend to be highly abstract, and they can often appear to have little relevance to the ordinary lives of believers. But theology at its best, and at its most authentic, is deeply embedded in the practice of faith.

This connection between theology and faith practices does not need to be created by complicated theological methods or by deep theoretical deliberation. Theology at its most basic is talk about God revealed in Jesus Christ. This gospel is always, everywhere, and variously held and communicated in and through the communal life of the church. Similarly, the church, simply through its normal activities, is deeply and profoundly theological. This is what Rowan Williams means by saying that theology does not have a starting point or a clear-cut methodological framework; it just has to start from where it is. Theological conversation grows out of and flows into the life of the church. By being part of the church and sharing in its life, believers are ordinary theologians. Practical theology, as its name implies, takes both theology and practice seriously. As Miller-McLemore argues, practical theology at its most basic is an everyday part of the life of Christian communities. So as believers share in practices such as remembering, absorbing, noticing, selecting/editing, and expressing, they are practical theologians.

Yet alongside these ordinary kinds of theologizing, there are more formal academic ways of doing practical theology. There is a discipline with academics holding appointments in colleges, universities, and seminaries; there are conversations around methods and ways of structuring teaching. This paraphernalia of academic life, however, finds its natural orientation and purpose in the life of the church. This is what Seward Hiltner called the "pastoral perspective" in theology. The pastoral perspective is not a theory; it comes out of the way that study and reflection arise from the joys and stresses of the practice of faith. So, by owning the reasons we are drawn to study, we move closer to the authentic nature of practical theology.

# 2

# Practical Theology as Faith Seeking Understanding

Definitions of practical theology are many and various. This will become very apparent as you read the chapters that follow. My own approach is, on the face of it, quite simple. I think of practical theology as a kind of theology that takes seriously both practice and theology. Taking both practice and theology seriously is not so much a definition as a rule of thumb that I use when I am planning a project, reading an academic book, or helping students with their work. In my mind, I am looking for something that is sufficiently practical while also being definitely theological. Taking practice and theology seriously should be obvious with something called practical theology, but the truth is that it is actually quite hard to achieve. It is possible for theology to ignore practice and as a result be almost entirely theoretical. That theology can have a blind spot when it comes to practice is not an unusual insight; indeed, some would argue that this is why practical theology is so important. But there is another common problem that is a little harder to detect. The problem is where something is called practical theology but does not appear on the face of it to be very theological at all. This is often the case, and it results in ways of thinking and writing that are at times more like religious studies, sociology, or political theory. So my rule of thumb is meant to be a corrective to these two tendencies: the tendency that theology might not really deal with practice (even when it says it does) and the possibility that practical theology can often fail to be theological (even when it thinks it is succeeding).

According to Saint Anselm, theology is "faith seeking understanding." This classic saying is particularly significant for practical theology because it carries within it a commitment both to the practice of faith and to theoretical reasoning. These two are joined by a third important strand where theological reasoning is understood as taking place within the context of spiritual life and prayer. This means that faith seeking understanding has within it a basic theological DNA that I think sets practical theology off on the right path. Faith seeking understanding therefore helps the task of doing practical theology because it combines a number of interrelated ideas that, when taken together, give a theological and a spiritual grounding to practical theology. Faith seeking understanding offers a theological framework for doing practical theology.

In this chapter I will explore the riches in this classic theological notion. It is, for some, a contentious move to make this connection between practical theology and faith seeking understanding. Some want to see practical theology as an academic discipline that should not be bound by particular forms of confession or religious commitments. While I respect that many within the discipline of practical theology understand their academic work in this way, it is not my approach in this book. Reasons for this arise from the particular kind of knowledge that theology implies—namely, that theology is the knowledge of God. It is this knowledge and its particular character as that which combines the practical, the theological, and the spiritual into a single whole that situates practical theology within the church and the life of faith.

## Faith in God

There are different understandings of practical theology. Some of these perspectives will be explored in more depth in the chapters that follow. While I accept that it is possible to do practical theology from a variety of religious perspectives, my own approach is situated in the Christian tradition. Adopting faith seeking understanding is my way of offering an approach to practical theology that takes theology seriously.

Practical theology as faith seeking understanding finds its primary orientation in the being of God. Faith is the perception of who God is, but it is also and most crucially a perception of what is given—given in the sense that it is gift, a work of faith in the believer, but also given in the sense that it is prior to faith. Indeed, the being of God is the condition for faith. So God, who is the creator of all things, of necessity exists before faith and precedes all forms of knowing. Practical theology seen as faith seeking understanding therefore starts from the realization that faith is faith in God. As a result, any kind of understanding that is sought is the understanding of God. This means faith is understood specifically as faith in God.

I advocate faith seeking understanding, then, as a way of orienting practical theology with the knowledge that within the Christian community there are a variety of different and competing ways of thinking about God. This variety of perspectives is evident, for instance, in the way theologians think about God as Trinity. Some want to replace the traditional language of Father, Son, and Holy Spirit with less gendered terms such as Creator, Redeemer, and Sustainer. God, it is felt, is not "he," and terms such as "fatherhood" and "sonship" support patriarchy. This is not the place to discuss the merits of either perspective. I mention this dispute because it illustrates a key dynamic in all theology. Theology is faith seeking understanding because all theological expression is to some extent provisional.

Theology is provisional because understanding God is not like other forms of understanding. This comes from the realization that God is not known in the way that other things are known. God is infinite, hidden from direct view, and ultimately beyond understanding. God is known only through God's own self-revealing. This is seen first and foremost in Jesus Christ. Christian theology is, therefore, the attempt to express the truth of Jesus Christ (the revelation of God) in human terms. Practical theology is the extension of this practice of expression into concrete, social, and cultural forms. Human expression is provisional, but God is not subject to or conditioned by understanding. The reality of God comes before and is beyond all expression and all knowing. This is precisely why theology is faith seeking understanding—expression is always to some extent culturally specific and subject to reinterpretation. This is the case even as God is beyond and not conditioned by human understanding.

## Faith Is Given

Knowing God is a work of the Holy Spirit in the believer. Faith seeking understanding makes this clear because it is only by faith that we share in the life of God. This is why faith is a gift as well as a human response to the divine. Practical theology understood as faith seeking understanding is oriented in such a way that knowing comes out of a relationship that exists for us before we even start to seek understanding. This relationship is the very basis for knowing. Faith seeking understanding is the continuation of that relational life. Faith, then, is not a departure point for practical theology but a characteristic of the way that practical theology is conducted. Practical theologian Ray Anderson has called this "Christopraxis." Christopraxis refers to the enterprise of practical theology as the ongoing work of Christ in the world through the power of the Holy Spirit.[1] For Anderson, the call to think theologically about practice is a missional sharing in the life of God. This echoes much earlier ways of thinking about theology as a mystical and salvific practice.

For the Greek fathers, theological knowledge conveyed the very life of God. Theology was not a theory but a mystical knowing and being known. This does not mean that it was anti-intellectual or theoretically simplistic; rather, it was understood as a way that the theologian shared actively in the life of God. It is mystical and spiritual in and through the processes of reasoning. For Origen, writing in the second century, knowledge of God was a spiritual rationality. True knowledge, in Origen's thinking, is communicated by God, and the "supreme instance" of this communication is the gospel. This "true" and "spiritual" knowledge is rooted in a mystical dialogue of encounter. "The knowledge of God," Origen says, "is God's bosom in which he places and holds all the God-minding persons as if they were his gold which he keeps in his bosom."[2] Origen's understanding of theology as a spiritual practice suggests a kind of practical theology based on an intimate encounter with God. It is an embrace or a mystical cradling close to the heart of God.

Faith seeking understanding carries within it the idea that the practice of theology is a relationship of trust and dependency. This is the recovery of more traditional ways of practicing theology within the Christian

---

1. Anderson, *Shape of Practical Theology*, 29.
2. Quoted in Dragas, *Meaning of Theology*, 17.

community. Theology here is a mark of belonging. We do practical theology because we are people of faith embraced by God. We are already in a relationship with God through Christ and through the work of the Holy Spirit. Faith seeking understanding describes what it means to be on the journey with God to continue to share in Christopraxis.

Yet as people of faith, we are seeking to gain further understanding. Faith is not a static position but a dynamic relational involvement in the life of God. Faith, then, is the fluid energizing that gives rise to the desire to seek understanding. This motivation comes from the life of God within the person setting out to do practical theology. Talking about practical theology as faith seeking understanding is, therefore, a way of accepting that knowledge of God is only possible within the relational dynamics of believing. This is a theological frame for practical theology that comes from who God is and what it means to know God.

## Faith, Knowing, and Creation

One objection to the approach I am suggesting is to say that while faith is key for salvation, practical theology is more concerned with practice. Practical theologians are interested in practical topics such as psychology and counseling, or leadership and church management, or politics and community development. These kinds of concerns, it could be assumed, require a different approach, one that draws on the social sciences, management theory, or political science. In response, I would argue that a theological approach to practical theology should avoid dividing knowledge such that theology sits apart from more secular or scientific ways of knowing. It should be emphasized that the interdisciplinary character of practical theology is not at all in dispute by advocating faith seeking understanding. The real issue is not with the utilization of insights, methods, and theoretical frameworks from disciplines other than theology but with the way that these are understood.

Faith seeking understanding does not just relate to the personal belief of the one doing practical theology; it also has significance for knowledge itself, whatever its source might be. As a result, it is important that interdisciplinary forms of practical theology require a theological approach to knowing. This way of thinking emphasizes that God precedes not only faith but also knowing and knowledge itself. This perspective has a long history in Christian tradition. An example is the Latin motto of the University of Oxford: *Dominus illuminatio mea* (the Lord is my light). The motto is taken from the first verse of Psalm 27, and it reflects a centuries-old theological understanding of knowledge. "The Lord is my light" is a reminder that reason, learning, and knowing find their source in the knowledge of God. The light that illuminates understanding and reason has its source in God, so all knowledge has its origins in the light of God. Such an approach does not just apply theology to social science; rather, it takes theology as the basis for true science, history, social science, and every form of human reason. Theologically, knowledge and reason have their origins in God because of creation. In the Letter to the Colossians, the writer sets out a vision of the universe where all things find their origin, redemption, and fulfillment in Christ.

> He is the image of the invisible God, the firstborn of all creation; for in him all things in heaven and on earth were created, things visible and invisible, whether thrones or dominions or rulers or powers—all things have been created through him and for him. He himself is before all things, and in him all things hold together. He is the head of the body, the church; he is the beginning, the firstborn from the dead, so that he might come to have first place in everything. For in him all the fullness of God was pleased to dwell, and through him God was pleased to reconcile to himself all things, whether on earth or in heaven, by making peace through the blood of his cross. (Col. 1:15–20)

Faith seeking understanding recognizes that both knowledge and knowing find their source in Christ. This comes from the relationship that everything created has to the being of God. There are important consequences with this kind of theological approach to reasoning. With its focus on practice, practical theology will almost inevitably be interdisciplinary. This means that different academic disciplines and kinds of reasoning and theory will generally be used alongside theological ways of thinking. Faith seeking understanding is a way of ordering knowledge theologically such that all things, including academic disciplines, are regarded as having their origins in Jesus Christ.

## Faith Seeking—Knowing and Not Knowing

Faith as a starting point for practical theology does not imply that belief is somehow set in stone. Faith is not a clear and defined set of doctrines, or at least it should not be taken solely as such. Doctrine and theology play their part, but they are situated in the dynamic that accepts that there is more to be understood. Faith seeking understanding orients practical theology toward a more dynamic and fluid approach to faith. Faith seeking understanding therefore carries within it a paradox. Faith, on the one hand, suggests something that is known—known about God and known about life in relation to God. This understanding can undergo theological formulation. It can be expressed and examined. On the other hand, the fact that this faith is seeking understanding also embraces a kind of mystery. Faith is something that is to be explored and further understood. Knowing and being known by God is therefore something that can develop. Development, however, takes place out of what has been experienced. The relationship of faith between God and the believer forms the starting point for further exploration.

Faith, then, is not an end point. The reason for this lies in the object of faith. Theological understanding is never comprehensive. As I have already said, knowledge of God is always to some extent provisional because God is infinite and beyond understanding. Faith, then, is a place of knowing and being known that accepts that it is limited. At the same time, the impulse to know more and to delve deeper into God and how God is at work in the world shapes practical theology as a way of seeking. This seeking, however, takes place in and through faith. It is dependent on the work of God through the Holy Spirit in the one who is seeking. Anselm makes this clear when he speaks about the task of the theologian.

> Come now, insignificant man, leave behind for a time your preoccupations; seclude yourself for a while from your disquieting thoughts. Turn aside now from heavy cares and disregard your wearisome tasks. Attend for a while to God and rest for a time in him. Enter the inner chamber of your mind and shut out all else except God and whatever is of aid to you in seeking him; after closing the door think upon your God. Speak now, my heart, where and how to seek you, where and how to find you. If you are not here, Lord, where shall I seek you in your absence? But if you are everywhere, why do I not behold you in your presence? Surely you dwell in light inaccessible.[3]

3. Anselm, *Proslogion* 1.

These lines come from the start of Anselm's *Proslogion*, written in the late eleventh century and originally titled *Faith Seeking Understanding*. The idea that theology starts with prayer and contemplation gives significant insight into how Anselm understood faith seeking understanding. Here the theologian is dependent on God for the act and process of theologizing. *Proslogion* is an extended argument concerning the existence of God. In it Anselm develops the ontological argument, which, in short, is the argument that God can be said to exist because humans carry in their minds the idea of "that than which no greater can be conceived." This knowledge, Anselm argues, demonstrates that such a being exists. This argument has been variously received and developed, but what is interesting here is that in what is a philosophical discussion concerning the existence of God and the use of reason in theology, Anselm starts with prayer. His prayer, however, seems to accept the existence of God even as he is rationally wrestling with this reality.

There has been a long-standing tradition in the Christian church that prayer is part of the theologian's calling. Toward the end of the fourth century, the monk Evagrius of Pontus said that the theologian is the one who prays truly, and the one who prays truly is a theologian.[4] Here theological reasoning and the practice of Christian spirituality are seen as mutually enriching. Practical theology seen as faith seeking understanding also holds together the practice of faith because the act of seeking understanding involves throwing oneself on God. Thus prayer is a kind of spiritual discipline that is fundamental to practical theology. The reason for this is that knowing is not something that takes place apart from or outside of God. Knowing arises from faith even as that faith is recognized as needing to be developed and further understood. Faith seeking understanding is an attitude that turns to God to be taught.

Seen in this way, practical theology is an act of faith where the act of seeking is actually a desire to be taught. So the theologian is one who by faith is taught how to seek. This is a journey of the heart that requires us to learn, through prayer, how to search for God and how to find God. Faith seeking understanding suggests that practical theology is best seen as a deep and enduring spiritual practice. The basis for seeking lies not primarily in theological method, although this will have its place, nor does

4. Evagrius of Pontus, *Chapters on Prayer* 60.

it lie in particular forms of reason or theory, though these also will have a place; rather, it lies in an orientation toward God. Such an orientation arises from prior theological and faith commitments, but it is on a path toward further understanding and exploration. Even this act of seeking is a dynamic that comes from faith. Knowing takes place within the divine life through the work of the Holy Spirit.

## Faith and Understanding as a Way of Life

Faith is always embodied and communal. One way to illustrate how this works is to look at ideas of culture. Sociologist Peter Berger spoke about the three dynamics of culture in relation to individuals. Culture, he says, is first experienced as something external to us.[5] We learn language and customs as part of the social reality into which we are born. Culture therefore has a reality outside of us to which we need to become accustomed. Without learning how things work, we are not able to operate as individuals in society. Culture, however, does not stay outside of us. Processes of education and socialization mean that what is external becomes internalized (Berger's second dynamic). These processes are so profound that internalized cultural forms merge with our own sense of ourselves such that it can be very difficult to imagine ourselves apart from this internal cultural conditioning. The third dynamic is the point at which the individual, through his or her creativity, contributes to culture more widely. This expression comes only as a consequence of the culture as an external reality and then as a socialized form of internal identity. This three-stage cultural dynamic can be used to illustrate how faith seeking understanding takes place.

The Christian faith is always handed down to us. Faith is a communal deposit. Whether we come to it through being born into a Christian family or through conversion, the cultural forms and expressions of faith will always be external to us. This cultural expression of faith has a social reality that is prior to our own believing. One way or another, then, we are born into faith. This insight is an important corrective for practical theology. It guards against any tendency to put theological reflection in a historical vacuum. Theology—and here practical theology is no exception—takes

5. Berger, *Social Reality of Religion*, 13–15.

place in relation to the ongoing life of the Christian community and the cultural expression of that community both in the present and over time. As Christians, we are inheritors of the faith. We become Christian and live as Christians in a community that is not simply in the present but also in the past.

Tradition, however, is not unified or univocal. There are different voices and opinions within the wider Christian community. We carry this varied tradition with us as identity. I belong to the Church of England, which means that I have been shaped by a particular expression of the faith. This is conveyed to me by the words we use in worship, the buildings we meet in, and the ways that Anglicans think and make decisions. If I had been raised as Christian in an independent church or in the Roman Catholic Church, the tradition that I would have inherited and been shaped by would have been different.

These differences are not simply denominational in nature. Christian traditions shift and alter between cultures and in different contexts. This insight has become more important in practical theology with the rise of contextual theology, such as Latino/a theology (or Dinka theology in India or the development of African and Asian theology). But focusing on the differences between denominations or contextual theologies does not tell the whole story. Alongside the variety, Christian tradition has significant continuities. The Bible is, for instance, a common source for Christian theology and thinking, whatever the church or cultural environment. The centrality of Jesus Christ is also a continuity, as is the use of bread and wine in worship.

These continuous elements, while they are interpreted in very different ways, are still a sign that the Christian tradition has both unifying and diverse aspects within it. We think out of, from within, and sometimes over and against these traditions. This work of connecting and reconnecting over the centuries is a way to work with ideas from the past and reconsider how they have influenced the present for both good and ill. This work is important because every community and each individual believer has been shaped and formed by church tradition.

Composer Gustav Mahler is often credited with saying, "Tradition is not guarding the ashes but fanning the flames." In other words, tradition has a place in theological thinking because it is alive and continues to be made alive. Practical theology has a vital part to play in fanning the flames by continually making connections between the voices of Christian communities and thinkers in the past and in the present-day life of the church. Tradition, by making use of voices not simply from the present but also from the past, thus offers ways of thinking and reflecting that draw on the wisdom of the church over the ages. These perspectives are a creative source for thinking in new ways. This approach to tradition sees the wisdom of the historical church as a treasure trove that is there to be rediscovered and made use of in the present. Tradition also is there as an authority in the Christian church.

In this chapter I have used Anselm as a guide for how we should think theologically. Of course there is no self-evident reason that Anselm should be used in this way, other than my own sense that what he is saying has significance. I am influenced in my choice of faith seeking understanding as a definition of theology because it is an approach to thinking theologically that has been part of the Christian church for almost a thousand years, but this in itself does not give this idea merit over any other. In other words, the present-day practical theologian makes choices about what to use and what not to use. It is through these choices that tradition evolves and is made fluid.

Tradition is often seen as being something of a problematic idea in practical theology. Many argue that theology as it has typically been practiced has marginalized and ignored particular groups. This is a key insight. No idea of tradition can be introduced without recognizing that traditions are constructed by those who have power. As a result, the Christian church has, for instance, prioritized male voices over female. Similar issues of power are seen in the marginalization of people of color and those who are economically and socially disadvantaged in society. This reality does not negate the basic point that tradition shapes both faith and understanding. It does, however, create a discussion around what should be emphasized and what should be downplayed in tradition. This debate is important precisely because tradition is central to thinking theologically and to our sense of ourselves as theologians and as part of the Christian community.

# 3

# The Gospel and
# Practical Theology

"I went to the crossroad / fell down on my knees." This is how blues singer Robert Johnson sang about his mythical encounter with the devil in "Cross Road Blues."[1] The song forms a central part of the legend that attributes Johnson's miraculous guitar playing to a Faustian pact he made at the crossroads. Johnson's virtuosity on the guitar is undeniable, and it has inspired a whole generation of rock and blues artists, but Johnson's pact with the devil plays into a wider narrative in African American culture concerning profane and secular forms of music. In *The Spirituals and the Blues*, theologian James Cone explores the relationship between the explicitly religious music of the African American church, known as the spirituals, and the music of the juke joints and bars, known as the blues. Cone rejects the idea that there is a divide between sacred and profane in these two forms of black music, arguing that both should be regarded as religiously significant because they speak of the historic experience of longing and oppression among African Americans.

The spirituals offer explicitly theological themes, drawing on biblical material and the language of the church, but they do this out of the

1. Robert Johnson, "Cross Road Blues," recorded November 27, 1936, released May 1937, on *Ramblin' on My Mind*, Vocalion, 10-inch 78 rpm.

39

experience of slavery and oppression. The blues speak of the yearning and paradox of African American experience. Cone's point is that these two musical forms should be read together rather than in opposition. It is not at all the case that one is sacred and the other of the devil; rather, they are two sides of the same coin. As Cone puts it, "Black music is unity music. It unites the joy and the sorrow, the love and the hate, the hope and the despair of black people; and it moves the people toward the direction of total liberation. It shapes and defines black existence and creates cultural structures for black expression."[2] Robert Johnson's "Cross Road Blues" exemplifies the experience of marginalization among African Americans at the start of the twentieth century. "Standin' at the crossroad / I tried to flag a ride / didn't nobody seem to know me / everybody pass me by." Some argue that the lyrics of the song do not really support the idea of a meeting with the devil, yet in the popular imagination this notion persists even when the first verse so clearly sets the whole experience within an explicitly Christian spirituality. Johnson says he fell down on his knees and "asked the Lord above 'Have mercy, now / save poor Bob, if you please.'" This observation takes us deep into the complexity of the blues, where spirituality and the experience of despair, sex, and booze coexist. This complex mix, however, is also echoed in the spirituals, where biblical themes carry dual meanings linked to resistance and escape for slaves.[3] Cone's reading of the spirituals and the blues comes from his understanding of the Christian gospel as liberation. Yet it is important to note that for Cone, the spirituals and the blues combine theological and biblical themes with the experience of life for African Americans. The gospel is evident precisely when these elements are held together, and this perspective offers a significant orientation to practical theology.

Theological work in the modern period has been characterized by a divide between theologians who prioritize doctrine and revelation and those who emphasize human experience as the source for knowledge of the divine. These positions have given rise to what have effectively been two opposing camps in theological work. On the one side is liberal theology, which has developed an agenda of adapting faith to the experience of contemporary life. On the other side is conservative theology, which has

2. Cone, *Spirituals and the Blues*, 5.
3. Ibid., 4.

focused on the interpretation of Scripture and the formulation of doctrine.[4] Modern theology can therefore be seen as a debate between the liberals and the conservatives. In between the two extreme positions are approaches that attempt to link or correlate theology and experience.[5]

This way of thinking about theology gives rise to a kind of mental map in which there is a straight line. At one end are experiential forms of theology, at the other end are doctrinal forms, and in between are a variety of correlational positions.[6] The mental map is important not simply because it shows a range of intellectual positions but also because it is a clue to the energy and emotions at stake in debates about theology. This energy comes from the deep belief held by those in opposing camps that what they are talking about is a theological truth. In other words, they have adopted their position in the belief that it gives them access to the theological truth of Jesus Christ. The gospel dimension to these positions is that they indicate the truth about God and Christ in human experience.

This dimension is what lies at the heart of James Cone's work on the spirituals and the blues. The African American experience, for Cone, carries a deep spirituality, and it therefore reveals an encounter with God. Cone then exemplifies an experiential (or liberal) emphasis in his work, and this leads to his understanding of the gospel as liberation for those who have been and are being oppressed. This perspective shapes how he approaches both the blues and the spirituals. It is an orientation that comes from how he understands the gospel in relation to experience. Cone's work is an example of how the gospel (and our understanding of it) fundamentally shapes contextual and practical theology.

I am using the idea of gospel here to speak about encounter with God and how that encounter is understood and communicated. The gospel understood in this way describes what is at stake in the choices we make as practical theologians. In this chapter, I explore the centrality of the gospel understood in this particular way through the work of two influential practical theologians—Bonnie Miller-McLemore and Andrew Root—who conceive of encounter with God, and hence the gospel, in quite different ways.

4. Stanley Grenz and John Franke have called this "foundationalism" (*Beyond Foundationalism*, 4).
5. See Tracy, *Blessed Rage*.
6. Ford, *Modern Theologians*, 2.

## Experience as the Site of Theological Inquiry

Bonnie Miller-McLemore is the editor of one of the key recent texts in practical theology, *The Wiley Blackwell Companion to Practical Theology*. Her work exemplifies the move within practical theology toward practice and human experience as the key field of inquiry. She sees her approach as disrupting the accepted methods and subject matter of theological inquiry. Practical theology, in contrast to biblical and systematic theology, pays attention to what she calls "the living web." Practical theology has been shaped, she argues, by the conviction that the living human document is a valid text for theological study, comparable to traditional texts of Scripture and doctrine.[7] Practical theology, then, is fundamentally oriented toward the everyday and the lived expression of communities. She explains the function of practical theology in this way:

> Its greater aim is to foster richer material understandings of embodied theology so that those who practice ministry and pursue lives of Christian faith will have a greater sense of their theological and religious vocation. Practical theology has always been and remains far more than an academic endeavor. It has been about returning theology to the people. As a discipline, practical theology is indeed secondary to the work and practice of most Christians and scholars. But as a way of faithful discipleship and as a way of doing theology in daily life, it is fundamental to Christian faith and to all areas of theological study and practice.[8]

Miller-McLemore's study of children and child-rearing reexamines culturally received notions of childhood and the role that Christian tradition has played in shaping these conventions. She argues for a revisionist understanding of childhood and parenthood as a prelude to changes in practice.[9] She draws on a feminist-maternal theology to reexamine the experience of childhood. This theology, first developed in her book *Also a Mother*, pays close attention to the experience of women as they engage in mothering and uses this as the basis for theology. There are four main premises for a feminist-maternal theology. First, it gives a privileged voice to the marginalized, which is extended to include women and children.

---

7. Miller-McLemore, *Christian Theology in Practice*, 1.
8. Miller-McLemore, "Five Misunderstandings," 26.
9. Miller-McLemore, *Let the Children Come*, xx.

Second, it challenges the "contradictory demonization and idealization of children and women's bodies in the acts of bearing and raising children."[10] Third, it enriches the debates about Christian doctrines such as love, sin, and grace by paying attention to the unequal relationship between adult and child. And finally, it stretches claims for justice and liberation beyond a call for sameness and identity based on the adult male. So Miller-McLemore's work is based on the view that God is revealed in and through the mundane and that liberation occurs in the commonplace: "in the embodied lives of children."[11] "Many feminist theologians have not only thought about children; they have acted as primary caregivers. Women may be enabled to hear children precisely because they have stood where children have stood, at the intersection of society's contradictory outward idealization and subtle devaluation of childcare and children."[12]

There is a theological blindness to children. "The presumed subject in theological treatises across the centuries has been the white European or European-American male adult."[13] But children and childhood have become more central in Western societies.[14] Children confound accepted models of spirituality and theology. So, for instance, the Methodist practical theologian James Fowler's stages of faith privilege the adult final stage.[15] Miller-McLemore writes,

> Knowing children challenge these conventional views and suggest the need for an expanded understanding of spirituality that embraces the whole of family living in all its beauty and misery. Their spirituality takes shape in the concrete activities of the day-to-day and the varied contexts where children and adults live together (e.g., playing, working, eating, talking, learning, fighting, reconciling, arriving, departing, and otherwise making a home). This is not to say that children rule out the importance of silence and solitude as part of the Christian life or that there are not important cognitive markers of faith's development. Rather children demand a widening of the circle of faith to include them more fully. Children actually exemplify a wisdom that somehow emerges in the chaos itself. In other words, children encourage us to reconsider ways in which spirituality for both children and

10. Ibid., xxxi.
11. Ibid., xxxii.
12. Ibid., xxi.
13. Miller-McLemore, "Feminism, Children, and Mothering," 7.
14. Ibid., 9.
15. Ibid., 15. See also the discussion of Fowler below in chap. 6.

adults takes shape in the midst of everyday rituals, practices, and habits that shape daily life.[16]

At stake in this move is a redistribution of power in terms of theological expression. The shift in power for Miller-McLemore is manifested primarily as a local concern.[17] As a result, she foregrounds everyday and localized activities such as what people wear, how they manage finances, and how they sing hymns. Quoting Charles Marsh's work on civil rights in Mississippi, she argues that this approach means that it is possible to inquire into the ways that people and places become "theaters of complex theological dramas."[18] Theology, she argues, "is more like liturgy. It is the *work of the people*, praising, arguing with, and turning to God in many contexts for diverse purposes."[19] Miller-McLemore describes her approach as a "low sacrificial Christology, high incarnation, non-creedal, non-patriarchal view of God."[20] God, she argues, can be "found anywhere God chooses. And I think God sometime favors trees and children."[21] Practical theology in the work of Miller-McLemore has moved beyond the idea of correlation between theology and experience or the study of beliefs and practice. Rather, she sets out to redefine what constitutes theological knowledge and pursues a theology that she argues is consequently inclusive and for the masses. Practical theologians, she suggests, are those who are "preoccupied with everyday concerns that evade and disrupt traditional categories, doctrines, and loci in theological and religious study."[22]

## Divine Action as Christopraxis

Miller-McLemore's work exemplifies a particular understanding of the knowledge of God, and hence it is a particular understanding of the gospel and how it is expressed and perceived in people's everyday lives. She prioritizes specific kinds of experience over doctrinal formulation. Andrew Root takes a diametrically opposed position. His work is also gospel focused,

16. Ibid., 15–16.
17. Miller-McLemore, *Christian Theology in Practice*, 4.
18. Marsh, *God's Long Summer*, 3, quoted in ibid.
19. Miller-McLemore, *Christian Theology in Practice*, 2.
20. Ibid., 19.
21. Ibid., 20.
22. Ibid., 18.

but his understanding of how God is encountered is markedly different from that of Miller-McLemore. Practical theology, Root argues, should be focused on divine action.[23] He is critical of practical theology, particularly as it has been practiced in the United States, and argues that the discipline has been very successful in analyzing and describing human action and experience but has largely failed to talk about divine action. The focus on the lived and embodied that characterizes much practical theology has meant that it has tended to be drawn to dialogue with philosophy, the social sciences, and empirical research. Divine action, however, has been regarded as being "impractical." By contrast, Root sets out to show that the work of God in the world touches people's lives and leads to transformation. The work of God "is not impractical, but rather is a deeply practical and lived reality, [and] people do have distinct experiences with God that they believe are concrete, lived, and *real*. These very experiences direct their lives in formative ways, moving them to do one thing or another in their embodied practical life" (*CP*, x). These experiences connect people to a reality that is beyond them. This is a transcendent realm that has become real and makes a difference in life.

Practical theology, Root says, should adjust its attention to take account of the experience of God in people's lives. Unfortunately, the discipline has tended to downplay divine action, and this has led to what he calls a "theological deficiency" (*CP*, x). "Practical theology has rightly started with people's experience, but because it has been blind to the possibility that people have *real* experiences with God, it has neglected to wade deeply into conceptions of divine action that would move practical theology further toward unique theological contributions." Central to Root's project is the notion of evangelical experience. By "evangelical" he means more than simply the experience of contemporary American evangelicals. He is appealing to a sensibility that goes back to the Reformation. This kind of experience is modeled by Martin Luther. As Root puts it, "By 'evangelical experience,' I mean the centrality of the commitment to a God who comes to us, calling each of us to confess our sin and follow the Jesus who lives" (*CP*, xi).

Root's understanding of experience is drawn from the theological concept of ministry. He suggests that Christ continues to minister in the

23. Root, *Christopraxis*, ix (hereafter cited in text as *CP*).

world through the work of the Holy Spirit. Root refers to this continuing ministry as "Christopraxis," a term that he draws from the work of his former teacher Ray Anderson. Christopraxis is the "criterion for practical theology itself, because it is the continuing action of Christ in the world" (*CP*, 90). This perspective is not simply a doctrinal position; it is also an experiential reality. Root illustrates this by drawing on a series of interviews in which his respondents shared their experience of God working in their lives. "People experience a real sense of God's action, of the praxis of Christ, and this experience is not simply intellectual or religious, but also personal and spiritual" (*CP*, 91). The work of Christ in the world precedes doctrinal formulation or theological reflection. It is the ministry of God's being coming to humanity. This ministry is God giving God's self to humanity, and as a consequence, humanity might then be with God (*CP*, 94). God's being is a dynamic or moved being that is revealed in ministry toward humanity. Theology comes from encountering the ministry of God.

At this point, Root draws on the work of German theologian Eberhard Jüngel. Jüngel develops a theological approach to ontology—that is, the being of God. Who God is—God's being—he argues, is God's becoming. In other words, as Root puts it, God is to be understood through the way that God ministers in the world. This perspective is fundamental to practical theology, first because theology is derived from the being of God as it is experienced through ministry, and second because "practice" is defined by the work of God in people's lives (*CP*, 95). Practical theology for Root is not primarily a discipline focused on interpreting human experience; rather, it is a field of study oriented toward the work of Christ in the world. So for Root, "Practical theology is the need to interpret the 'where' of Jesus Christ in our experiences of the now" (*CP*, 99).

Central to Root's argument is the conviction that there is a pattern that determines how the work of God can be discerned in the world. This pattern he calls "death-to-life" and "life out of death" (*CP*, 104). As a lens to see the work of God, this pattern comes from the being of God revealed in the world. "The divine and human are associated not through practices, culture, or even doctrine, but through death . . . and it is God's ministry to enter death" (*CP*, 105). To know God, then, is to die; this theology of the cross lies at the heart of Root's approach to practical theology. To encounter God is to be judged as being dead, for this is what we are. "We are weak, broken, and have no way of saving ourselves." It is only out of death that grace can be experienced. "Grace is the human experience of God's being as becoming in the ministry of bringing life out of death" (*CP*, 107). This work of God, Root argues, is to be understood through the Reformation doctrine of justification by faith. Jüngel uses this doctrine as a lens or an interpretative framework for practical theology (*CP*, 121). Justification is to be seen not so much as a legal concept but as a relational dynamic that operates between divine action and human action. So Root says, "I turn to justification as a way to embrace and explore human experience as the location for the encounter with God's own ministry of being in becoming" (*CP*, 123).

Root regards justification as the overarching doctrinal framework for understanding and perceiving the action of God in the world. This incorporates creation, where the Word brings forth being out of nothingness. Human sin is read as the denial of creaturely condition, the search for actuality rather than the acceptance of creaturely nothingness (*CP*, 128). The incarnation is the action of ministry in the world. Sin enters the world through the denial of the nothingness of humanity and the search for an actuality apart from God. Justification, by contrast, is the possibility to return that reinstates the position of being created out of nothing. This comes through God's "own act of ministry" (*CP*, 130–31). Supremely this comes through the death of Christ on the cross, where he enters nothingness, thereby bringing about salvation through his own perishing. "In the incarnation and crucifixion God's Word becomes flesh, reversing original sin, for as creation fell when creature tried to become creator, so now the Word that is God, the Word that creates out of nothing, the Word that is the Creator becomes creature" (*CP*, 131–32). This movement of ministry is the love of God for the world. Through the perishing of Christ on the cross, nothingness is turned into possibility. The resurrection turns human perishing into new life. "The resurrection turns perishing into possibility; it makes all concrete lived experiences of perishing the location of God's being as becoming and therefore paradigmatic to practical theology" (*CP*, 133).

## Gospel—a Way of Seeing

Bonnie Miller-McLemore and Andrew Root represent two significant but contrasting voices in practical theology. Miller-McLemore emphasizes the experience of those marginalized in society over formal doctrinal formulation as the source for theological insight. This is a classically liberal approach to theology. Root, on the other hand, works from a predetermined doctrinal position based on justification by faith. From this theological understanding he develops a lens to view the lived practice of faith. This is a traditionally conservative position. Miller-McLemore and Root therefore can be seen as coming from opposite ends of the spectrum that has shaped the modern theological landscape. Yet while there are quite fundamental differences between these two practical theologians, these differences come out of a desire to speak about the work of God in the world. Put in my terms, they both orient their work around the gospel, but they understand this gospel in different ways.

For Root, the gospel is articulated explicitly in specifically doctrinal terms. Justification by faith becomes an interpretative tool that Root says offers an insight into the work of God in the world. Thus he can talk about the paradigm of death to life and life to death that is the mark of divine action. Miller-McLemore's approach is less clearly articulated, but it is nevertheless a theological understanding of the gospel that shapes her approach to practical theology. For Miller-McLemore, it is in the experience of motherhood, in everyday life, and in particular in the context of children that God is most vividly present. It is important, however, to note that Miller-McLemore is also interested in divine action in the world, and she sees theological insight as developing out of this perception of the divine. Her work is focused on children and motherhood precisely because this is her understanding of the good news as it is made evident in the lived and the experiential.

I have talked at length about these two practical theologians because their work exemplifies one of the central issues in practical theology: What is the gospel? The answer to this question is fundamental in practical theology because our understanding of the gospel creates the lens for practical theology. "Gospel" as I am using it here is more than doctrine or theology. Gospel refers to the work of God in the world and how this work is understood and experienced. Gospel is much more than a message about Jesus Christ; it describes the life sparked by this message. Gospel is therefore different from theology. A theology is an abstract set of ideas. Gospel combines an understanding of God with the embodied and committed lives of individuals.

Gospel, then, requires an investment. But investment is not simply a social or personal action of Christians and communities. The gospel also includes divine action in the church and the world. This is why it lies at the heart of practical theology and why different understandings and experiences of the gospel shape practical theology in different ways. Practical theology is a way of reasoning about how the work of God in the world is experienced and understood. Doing practical theology thus cannot be separated from a consideration of the gospel because this forms the lens that fundamentally shapes how it is to be conducted. In the next section I will develop an understanding of the gospel that can shape practical theology. In John's Gospel there is a clue to how it is possible to move beyond the mental map of modern theology that divides approaches between liberal and conservative.

## John's Gospel and the Gospel

The debate within practical theology about divine action has pivoted around two opposing positions: the liberal, which argues that divine encounter is understood in and through experience, and the conservative, which prioritizes doctrine. So far I have argued that these are in effect different ways of understanding the gospel. John's Gospel, I want to suggest, gives an alternative perspective that can be used to reframe the conversation, collapsing the differences between these two opposing camps.

In John's Gospel, the truth is a person, not a set of doctrines or an experience. So when Jesus says "I am the way, and the truth, and the life" (John 14:6), he seems to wrong-foot our expectation that the truth will be something we can grasp intellectually and make sense of with rational processes, whether as doctrine or indeed as an account of experience. Truth is embodied in the person of Jesus. This shouldn't be a surprise. We have already been told in the opening chapter of John's Gospel that Jesus is the one who was with God and who came from God. He is the Word.

Yet, interestingly, Jesus as the truth is linked in this "I am" saying with the way and the life. Way and life both carry the sense of something that is in process—that is, an embodied experience in the world. Life is something that is lived out, and a way is something that you journey along. The truth appears to be not so much something that we find out but something that takes us on a journey. Yet this journey and this life are also identified with Jesus. The "truth" is not something that is capable of being neatly defined. In fact, it seems that in John's Gospel being puzzled is part of being on the *way* and of experiencing the *truth*. Trying to make sense of things is therefore essential to the *life*.

This dynamic can be illustrated by looking at Nicodemus's encounter with Jesus in John's Gospel. Meeting Jesus and hearing him speak was no guarantee of understanding. In fact, encounters with Jesus in John's Gospel were just as likely to confuse and provoke misunderstanding as understanding. When Nicodemus comes to him, Jesus seems determined to confuse and perplex. Nicodemus is a Pharisee and a leader of the Jews (John 3:1). He visits Jesus by night, perhaps because he wanted to keep his interest in the controversial teacher discreet. He says, "Rabbi, we know that you are a teacher who has come from God; for no one can do these signs that you do apart from the presence of God" (John 3:2–3).

Just as at the cleansing of the temple, the question of Jesus's identity and authority is framed around signs, but Jesus doesn't get into the discussion in quite the way that Nicodemus expects. He doesn't affirm or indeed seem to welcome Nicodemus's apparent confession of faith. Jesus responds by saying that "no one can see the kingdom of God without being born from above." It is not possible to enter into God's kingdom "without being born of water and Spirit. What is born of the flesh is flesh, and what is born of the Spirit is spirit" (John 3:3, 5–6).

Nicodemus is even more confused by this response. He is taken by Jesus to the edge of a deep mystery of new life in relation to God. The idea of being "born again" has become a key identity marker for many Christians. We think we know what we mean when we talk about being born again. This certainty, however, passes over the deep mystery that Jesus opens up to Nicodemus, that salvation involves the work of the Spirit bringing a completely new life into being.

It is in this context that John speaks about the love of God and the gift of the Son in verse 16. John 3:16 has for many become the archetypal biblical summary of the gospel: "For God so loved the world that he gave his only Son, so that everyone who believes in him may not perish but may have eternal life." John places this saying in the context of the conversation with Nicodemus about being born again by the Spirit. Belief therefore is deeply connected to the inward work of God in the believer.

The gospel in John's Gospel, then, has a twin dynamic. The gospel message of the way and the truth and the life finds its origin and content in the person of Jesus Christ. This means that theological expression of the gospel depends on a close correspondence to the person of Jesus Christ revealed in the Scriptures. So when we ask what the way is, or how to live the life, or how to find truth, the answer is Jesus Christ.

Doctrine, then, is always relative to the rich and deep complexity of the Word. At the same time, the truth of Jesus Christ is apprehended by personal transformation, being born again of the Spirit. In other words, belief is never simply the acceptance of doctrinal formulation about Jesus Christ. The truth is not understood or indeed accepted as fact, because this truth is a person, Jesus Christ, who comes to us through the work of the Spirit.

## Gospel-Based Practical Theology

The most important decision that anyone setting out to do practical theology has to resolve is, what is the gospel? In this chapter I have shown how two practical theologians deal with this issue and how their understanding of the work of God in people's lives shapes how they approach their work. Bonnie Miller-McLemore and Andrew Root represent two ends of the spectrum in practical theology. As such, I think they represent what might be called a liberal and a conservative voice in the discipline.[24] The liberal voice emphasizes experience over doctrine, and the conservative prioritizes doctrine over experience. These two different approaches are well-worked theological ways of operating, and they can be a little like tramlines or ruts in the road, in that they can capture the way we go about doing practical theology. Whichever line we get drawn into seems to determine the way forward. It is also important to see that these ways of thinking carry deep conviction. They arise from firmly held views about how God works in the world, and as such their advocates adhere to them as gospel.

24. I argue this with the realization that both Miller-McLemore and Root might object to the way I have presented their work. I think they would argue that they want, in their different ways, to overcome the liberal/conservative divide. I would accept that perhaps they do not represent the extremes of the two ends of the theological mental map as I have represented them and that each seeks to develop a connection between theology and experience. They are then both perhaps more correlational in approach, albeit at different ends of the correlational spectrum.

The gospel orientation, however, suggests an important corrective to the polarized divisions between liberal and conservative. Using John's Gospel, I have argued that the gospel, while it may be expressed as doctrine, is never simply ideas. The gospel is Jesus Christ. When we as Christians try to express our faith, it is always an attempt to frame in words something that is beyond expression.

This does not mean that all theological expression is pointless. In fact, the opposite is the case. The point is that as we speak the gospel we are speaking of a truth that is a person. This means that claims to be able to see the work of God cannot come from doctrinal correctness or sophistication but from relationship with Christ. Doctrine might attempt to clarify or express this perspective, but it is not a place from which to generate security, because the truth is not an idea or a way of reasoning but a person.

The same kind of dynamic is also operative in relation to the experience of faith by the believer. Here the gospel is also relational, and rather than providing a sure place for reasoning, it simply opens up mystery. The wind can be felt, but ultimately we don't know where it comes from or where it goes. Becoming a creature born anew is an experience, but it cannot be the sole basis for reasoning or rational inquiry into the work of God. Rather, the experience points to the relational presence of the Holy Spirit in human experience.

A gospel perspective is basic in practical theology because the gospel speaks of how we understand God to be at work in the world. I recognize that each of us may have different ways of thinking about the work of God. My intention is not so much to argue for one way of understanding the gospel over another; rather, I want to point out, on the one hand, the possible limitations that come from opting for either the liberal or the conservative line and to point toward, on the other hand, the need for these perspectives to be held together.

Each of us will need to take a view on the relationship between experience and doctrine and where we place the emphasis. This is important in the first instance when you are doing your own work, but it is also important when you are reading the work of others. So if you are reading a book or an article by a practical theologian, the most important question to ask is, how does this person conceive of the gospel? Both the liberal and the conservative positions ultimately reduce the complexity of the gospel.

The relational dynamics that I have introduced from John's Gospel do not in themselves solve the problem of the divide between experience and doctrine. But as I have argued in the previous chapter, every expression of the gospel will fall short of the truth of Jesus Christ. This does not mean we should not try to express this message or indeed take it as a guide to develop practical theological insights. What it means is that we will need to continually return to Jesus Christ as he is seen in the Scriptures to regulate and revise how we are speaking and thinking. This is precisely what is meant by "faith seeking understanding."

# 4

# Practical Theology and Lived Theology

One of the most exciting new developments in practical theology is the energy that has been generated from theology as it is embodied and lived by individuals and in communities. This is an emerging field of study in which different and competing ideas and theories are used to describe a shared phenomenon.[1] Here I will focus on three main approaches. The first will be the idea of lived religion, drawing on the work of David Hall, Meredith McGuire, and Robert Orsi. The second will be Jeff Astley's concept of ordinary theology, and the third will be the four voices of theology theory that has been developed by Helen Cameron and her colleagues in the ARCS (Action Research: Church and Society) project.

1. The move toward the ordinary in practical theology is part of a much wider turn to the subject and to practice in the study of religion. But as with any emerging areas, this turn has led to a contested field of different terms. In the 1980s, Grace Davie introduced the idea of "common" religion (see Ahern and Davie, *Inner City God*, 32). At the same time, Robert Schreiter spoke about local theologies (*Constructing Local Theologies*). In the history of religion, writers such as Karen Louise Jolly explored different aspects of "popular religion" (*Popular Religion in Late Saxon England*). The term "popular religion" was also shared by those in religious studies and by Roman Catholic theologians (see, e.g., De Luna, *Faith Formation and Popular Religion*, and Maldonado, "Popular Religion," 3–11). For a more recent work in this area, see Gortner, *Varieties of Personal Theology*.

What these different ways of thinking have in common is the notion that theology as it is expressed and lived in ordinary communities coexists with and in part depends on—but is also at times in tension or even in contradiction with—more institutional or formal kinds of theology. This means that in a congregation, for instance, there may be the official theology that is expressed by the minister or by the worship, and then there may be a whole range of different personal theologies that individuals live their lives by.

Exploring the relationship between these different kinds of theology has become the focus of a variety of exciting research and writing projects across the theological and social scientific disciplines. If practical theology is a way of thinking that takes seriously both practice and theology, this area of the lived or ordinary and embodied is one of the most important places to give our attention to, because it is where practice and theology are most fundamentally and organically interconnected.

This chapter, therefore, charts an understanding of practice and theology. At the end I argue that the idea of lived theology (as distinct from lived religion, as we will discuss below) brings the three approaches together in a way that can help those of us working in practical theology.

## Lived Religion

The idea of lived religion has its origins in French sociology. It has been taken up by a range of scholars working in the study of religion, where it has been developed as a cultural or ethnographic approach to researching and understanding religious practice.[2] Lived religion is closely linked to the notion of practice. David Hall speaks about practice as the choice that individuals take to act. Lived religion is akin to the idea that culture is enacted or performed through practices.[3] This means that lived religion needs to be understood as something that is incomplete and provisional. To quote the French sociologist Danièle Hervieu-Léger, it is "fluid, mobile, and incompletely structured."[4] Religion that is lived is not set in stone or circumscribed; rather, it is on the move. As Robert Orsi says, "All religious ideas and impulses are of the moment, invented, taken, borrowed, and improvised at the intersections of life."[5]

2. Hall, introduction to *Lived Religion in America*, vii.
3. Ibid., xi.
4. Hervieu-Léger, "'What Scripture Tells Me,'" 22.
5. Orsi, "Everyday Miracles," 8.

Research into religion can therefore never be simply a discussion of ideas or doctrines. Lived religion requires that time is taken to pay close attention to the experiences of ordinary believers and how they live their lives in relation to religion. Beliefs, it is argued, must be "activated" and made alive by people if they are to be understood for their true significance. It is in this context that the theologizing of individuals should be understood.

Theologies are generated in a range of different venues—in the streets, in homes, in churches—and they operate in relation to formal and informal conceptions of God. This means that there is a dynamic and ongoing relationship between, on the one hand, theology that develops and exists as part of everyday experience and, on the other hand, the influence and power of religious authorities.[6] Lived religion is therefore characterized by what Orsi calls hybridity. In other words, religion in the everyday is quite likely to be a mixture of different and even contradictory perspectives. Hybridity points to the ways in which, for some individuals, different religious practices and perspectives can coexist. So, for example, a Christian minister may also practice Buddhist meditation, or a charismatic Christian might go on an Ignatian retreat.

Hybridity is common in lived religion in ways that seem incoherent at the level of formal or theological thought. This is then a cultural approach to theology that takes account of how religion and culture embed the religious person and community in history. Orsi's approach recognizes that culture is not something that religious communities are "in" so much as something that is necessary to express their identity and develop their way of life.[7] It is this cultural perspective on religion that structures how practices should be understood.

Working in sociology of religion, Meredith McGuire has further developed the conception of lived religion. McGuire is concerned to make a distinction between an understanding of religion that prioritizes the perspectives of what she calls "official spokespersons" and one in which "religion and spirituality [are] practiced, experienced, and expressed by ordinary people."[8] Lived religion has developed as a way of speaking about religion that is not primarily cognitive or doctrinal in orientation.

6. Ibid., 11.
7. Ibid., 16.
8. McGuire, *Lived Religion*, 12.

As a consequence, religious belief is not to be seen primarily as some-thing to do with a person's mind or thinking. Religion is rather a close mix of belief and practice, and this mix functions in a social setting.[9] Religion, according to Robert Orsi, is "the practice of making the invisible visible, of concretizing the order of the universe, the nature of human life and its destiny, and the various dimensions and possibilities of human interior-ity itself, as these are understood in various cultures at different times, in order to render them visible and tangible, present to the senses in the circumstances of everyday life."[10]

This approach to religion means that belief is encountered and ex-perienced in bodies as well as in ideas. As a result, religious rituals and practices become central to the analysis because these make the invisible present in embodied experiences. Practices are ways in which individuals and communities become connected to the spiritual. McGuire argues that lived religion, because it is based on practices rather than ideas or beliefs, does not necessarily have to be logically coherent or consistent. Instead, it demands what she calls a practical coherence. In other words, it has to form a logical whole for the participant, but this logic might appear to be irrational or even superstitious to the outside observer.

Lived religion may not accord with the ways that formal belief is con-stituted by religious institutions; in fact, the idea of consistency in belief might be much less of a priority for ordinary believers than it is for academics or for professional ministers of religion. Most people, Mc-Guire observes, are not very interested in achieving consistency between "their wide-ranging beliefs, perceptions, experiences, values, practices, and actions." Lived religion is much more likely to be characterized by complexity, apparent inconsistency, heterogeneity, and a basic untidiness around the range of practices and ideas that people find helpful in their daily lives.[11]

## Ordinary Theology

Lived religion as a concept has developed primarily within the social sci-ences. At the same time, there has been a growing interest in practical

9. Ibid., 13.
10. Orsi, *Between Heaven and Earth*, 73–74.
11. McGuire, *Lived Religion*, 16.

theology in what has been called ordinary theology.[12] Ordinary theology is a theory of personal or individual theology that was first developed by practical theologian Jeff Astley.[13] Astley defines ordinary Christian theology as "the theology and theologizing of Christians who have received little or no theological education of a scholarly academic or systematic kind."[14] The focus of interest is on what Astley calls the "God-talk" of believers—a way of describing the kinds of theological reflection that are characteristic of Christians who have not participated in theological education.[15]

Cognitive reflection for Astley is not a denial of the importance of practice; rather, it arises from the opaque and hidden nature of religious experience. He argues that it is difficult to infer beliefs from practice. One reason for this is that there is rarely a one-to-one correlation between beliefs and their expression in action. Hence he argues that "different theologies may undergird the same practice, and we must be cautious about imputing to people's practice a theology that they would not themselves claim to hold." Ordinary theology therefore focuses on listening to what people are saying. The focus on people's God-talk is important because it is hard to discern the theology that is implicit in what people do. "However hesitant, inarticulate and unsystematic is a person's ordinary theology, it is easier literally to hear than is their practice. Practice speaks 'very loudly,' of course, as we say; and often 'more loudly than words.' But it does not speak *in words*. Inferring people's theology from their practice may sometimes be our only recourse; but it is rather a different sort of activity from describing, understanding and analysing what they say."[16]

Ordinary theology is transmitted in different ways than those usually associated with the university or the seminary. It is the theology that all believers start with and learn first.[17] Ordinary theology is passed on by acts of prayer and worship. It is learned in Bible study groups, in Christian fellowship, and through the everyday experiences of life in the home and in

12. See Christie, *Ordinary Christology*; Village, *Bible and Lay People*; and Cartledge, *Testimony in the Spirit*.

13. Astley, *Ordinary Theology*; Astley and Christie, *Taking Ordinary Theology Seriously*; and Astley and Francis, *Exploring Ordinary Theology*.

14. Astley, *Ordinary Theology*, 56.

15. Astley, "Analysis, Investigation and Application of Ordinary Theology," 1.

16. Ibid., 5–6.

17. Ibid.

the community.[18] Ordinary theology is a lay theology, says Astley, because it is shared by the whole people of God. This is the theology that runs like a thread through people's lives, and it exists in the web of relationships that constitute communities.

Astley and coauthor Ann Christie argue that this kind of theology matters because it does work for people.[19] Technical language and terms are generally not very useful in everyday contexts, and as a result, ordinary theology does not make use of complex or highly abstract concepts. This does not mean that there is no depth or profound insight to be found in ordinary theology. The seriousness of ordinary theology is a "feature of personal avowal rather than of scholarly learning."[20] Academic theology is the preserve of the scholarly few and as such is a minority interest compared to the vast majority of Christians who live their lives out of and through ordinary ways of thinking theologically. Ordinary theology is therefore primarily a working theology, and as a result, it is not a slight or inconsequential topic. Ordinary theology really matters to people.[21]

Ordinary theology is important, Astley argues, because the church needs to know how believers habitually think and how they receive the ongoing teaching ministry of the clergy and other ministers.[22] This means that every minister, teacher, or pastoral worker in a church needs to be familiar with the ordinary theology of the people with whom he or she works in the local community. Success in ministry necessitates a thorough understanding and ability to relate to ordinary theology.[23]

The focus on ordinary believing requires a turn toward empirical methods in theology because there is no other way to uncover this phenomenon. Ordinary theology and lived religion share this imperative to adopt empirical forms of research and inquiry.

## The Four Theological Voices

The four theological voices method of research has been developed by the ARCS team (Helen Cameron, Deborah Bhatti, Catherine Duce, James

18. Ibid., 1.
19. Astley and Christie, *Taking Ordinary Theology Seriously*, 6.
20. Ibid., 6–7.
21. Ibid., 7.
22. Astley, "Analysis, Investigation and Application of Ordinary Theology," 2.
23. Astley and Christie, *Taking Ordinary Theology Seriously*, 5.

Sweeney, and Clare Watkins). The team developed its approach while working with churches, Christian NGOs, and organizations in the United Kingdom. The methodology is based on sustained empirical research that sets out to work with these partners to facilitate theological reflection. In *Talking about God in Practice*, the authors introduce the different theological voices that become evident through a careful examination of the practice of the church. These voices are mixed together in the everyday speech and action of communities, and as such they form a rich and living "whole."

In seeking to understand how theology is intertwined with action, they have developed an interpretative typology that helps them to identify different strands of theological communication in the life of the church. They see the voices typology as a "working tool." The tool is developed around the notion that in the lived practice of the church there are four theological voices: operant theology, espoused theology, normative theology, and formal theology.[24]

Cameron and the ARCS team argue that the fundamental starting point in the kind of research they do needs to be the realization that the practice of the church is theological. As Clare Watkins puts it, "Practices are bearers of theology."[25] This means that theology is somehow embodied in the practice of the church. Operant theology is the theology that is evident in how people act and embody faith. Operant theology is not generally something that is easily explained or described, they argue; rather, it needs to be uncovered and discovered by believers themselves because operant theologies are often slightly hidden from view or taken as "just the thing that we do." It is only when they are subjected to attention and reflection that these everyday ways of believing reveal their theological nature. The four voices method of analysis has come about because the researchers have found in their work with churches a particular tendency for there to be differences between the theology that is evident in practice and the theology that people articulate. Their term for theology that is articulated is "espoused theology."

Espoused theology is the theology spoken by the members of the church or organization. Cameron's team observed that among the churches studied, belief and believing appear to operate in a way that enables and occasionally supports subtle and at times confusing differences between what is stated and the underlying operant theology that works out in practice.

24. Cameron et al., *Talking about God in Practice*, 49–56.
25. Watkins, "Practical Ecclesiology," 169.

Espoused theology has its roots in the wider tradition and expression of the church. In other words, "Espoused theologies come from somewhere." Churches and believers develop their espoused theological understandings in relation to the ongoing teaching and theological understanding of their churches. So the theology that people speak about in relation to their practice is drawn from Scripture or liturgy or other theological and spiritual writings, as well as experience.[26]

The third theological voice, normative theology, is therefore used to show how these varied sources are often utilized as a guide and a corrective alongside practice both by communities and by believers. Here again it is possible to observe interesting and sometimes contradictory relationships between the normative voice in a community and the espoused theology of individual believers.

The final voice identified by Cameron's ARCS team is formal theology. This refers to the contribution academic or professional theologians bring to understanding the practice and the life of the church. This voice, however, is deeply entwined with the other three theological voices. Espoused and normative theology draw to varying degrees on formal theology.[27] A good example of this is the way that ministers continue to find inspiration from their studies at college when they preach or the extent to which believers engage with academic theology in their personal reading or when they attend Christian festivals and events.

The normative theology contained in the liturgy of the church is often influenced by the wider academic conversations that make up the formal theological voice. Alongside this embedded formal voice is a particular role that the ARCS team sees for academic engagement with practice. Academic theology offers a critical perspective on the lived expression of the church. It is able, when it is at its best, to "shine a light" on the actions of the church and the state of believing.

## Introducing Lived Theology

Lived religion, ordinary theology, and the four theological voices, while they are distinct and different, all describe a phenomenon that is crucially

26. Cameron et al., *Talking about God in Practice*, 53.
27. Ibid., 55.

important for practical theology. It is essential that we can give an account of theology as it is lived and experienced if, as practical theologians, we want to effectively and accurately reflect on the Christian community. These three approaches together offer important insights that should shape how we do practical theology. While they are very different, they can be combined to generate a way of working and seeing the life of the church, and indeed the wider society, that should be at the heart of how we approach practical theology.

Lived religion in some ways downplays theology as an adequate description of religious experience. In the place of doctrinal descriptions favored by religious institutions, lived religion focuses on individuals and groups as they engage in rituals and practices. Theology is not completely bracketed out by this approach, but it is seen as a part of this embodied and performed cultural environment. In other words, it is not given a privileged place as a form of overarching explanation.

Ordinary theology, by contrast, argues for theology as the key to understanding practice. Here, the focus is definitely on the speech of believers and the ways that they reason and understand using doctrinal formulation. Practice, it is argued by those who advocate ordinary theology, can only be understood through the words of those who participate. Observation cannot in and of itself take us into the minds of participants.

The four theological voices approach situates the expressed or espoused theology of ordinary believers in a more nuanced web of theological expression. It suggests that theological expression is not limited to speech but can also be found in actions. This kind of operant theology can be implicit, and ordinary believers may not be aware that it exists. Moreover, as opposed to the ordinary theology perspective, the four voices approach traces the ways in which both espoused and operant theologies exist in relation to more formal and normative voices. So instead of isolating ordinary theology as distinct and separate from more academic or formal kinds of theology, the four voices approach looks for the interrelationship of theological forms of expression that exist around communities and religious practice.

Despite the differences between these ways of conceptualizing the lived nature of religious practice and theology, all three have a valuable contribution to make. I am therefore suggesting a term that should be used for this combined approach: "lived theology."[28] Lived theology combines significant perspectives from lived religion, ordinary theology, and the four theological voices. This combined way of talking about theology as it is lived in communities needs to be at the heart of any form of practical theology. In the final part of this chapter, I will discuss the contribution that lived theology, as I have conceived it, can make to practical theology.

### Lived Theology Shapes Us as Practical Theologians

I have already discussed the way that faith seeking understanding means we are all shaped by our experience of the church. Lived theology is a way of giving expression to this as part of an overall approach to practical theology. Because we are all formed as theologians by the communities of which we are a part, lived theology has a powerful influence on how we approach practical theology. Lived theology is operant in us as a way of selecting and making decisions, and this dynamic is something that everyone brings to practical theology. As a result, lived theology directs our attention in such a way that it influences what we think and how we see things. This means that our viewpoint is to some extent already shaped before we start to do practical theology. This does not mean that the process of theological education will not influence how we think. The point is that as we learn, there is a process of developing and growing the theology that we already carry with us. There may be occasions when new insights and perspectives cause us to revise our thinking in fundamental ways, but our lived theology is the baseline for this process.

### Lived Theology Is the Starting Point for Practical Theology

It is almost impossible to do practical theology well without first reflecting on our own lived theology. There are a number of reasons for this. Most glaringly, if our lived theology shapes the way we look at life, then we need to give some time to reflecting on how exactly this works for each of us. This kind of self-examination might not be easy. The four voices approach makes it clear that there are several layers of theology at work in communities. These layers are also part of the makeup of each of us individually as believers. So we might have operant theology

28. "Lived theology" is a term that has also been adopted by Charles Marsh, Peter Slade, and Sarah Azaransky; see their edited volume *Lived Theology*.

that shapes the way we act and react. This kind of theology might be implicit in the things we do, and hence it can be hidden or obscured from our view.

Alongside our operant theology will be the theology that we speak and own. This theology will also be a part of our selves. The ordinary theology perspective suggests that this spoken theology is likely to be our primary and most deeply held perspective on life. I would add that this deep or inherent ordinary theology almost certainly combines the operant and the espoused. Lived theology shapes the way we pray and the way we choose to live our lives. Thus it is essential to spend time reflecting on our own lived theology when we set out to do practical theology, since it has such a deep influence on how we think and act as Christians—not only day-to-day but most crucially when we are in the process of trying to reflect theologically as practical theologians.

### Lived Theology Is Performed

Every Christian community carries within it a vibrant lived theology. Lived theology is enacted within the everyday practices of religious life and embodied in the way that individuals make and remake themselves through sharing in a religious world. There is, then, a fundamental performative element to lived theology. It is not simply spoken as an explanation; it is acted out, and this practice means it lives. Practical theological method must therefore be shaped in such a way that it is able to pay deep and close attention to the performance of theology in Christian communities and in the wider society.

### Lived Theology Is Complex

Within Christian communities, lived theology is multilayered. Lived theology exists in practices and religious rituals, but simultaneously it is also found in the way that individuals and groups think about these phenomena. Practical theology needs to pay attention to the various ways that thought and action coexist and have a deep interactive relationship with one another. To further complicate this picture, there will often be a number of different theological understandings that are part of the lived theology of any one Christian community. So there may be different formal theological accounts, there may be varied institutional accounts, and then there will be the many theologies that individuals express and make operant. All of these constitute lived theology in any one context.

### Lived Theology Can Be Contradictory

The multilayered nature of lived theology is further complicated by the fact that individuals can and in fact are quite likely to hold conflicting and contradictory theological perspectives. The reason for this is that we do not generally systemize our thoughts; rather, we develop them in relation to the events of life. One of the consequences of this way of generating lived theology is that we do not normally worry much about consistency or coherence. Lived theology is primarily concerned with doing what is right and being faithful in particular circumstances.

### Not All Lived Theology Is Good

Practical theology is essential for the church because communities from time to time generate forms of lived theology that are problematic. Lived theology is part of the cultural flow of society, and as a result it can easily develop in ways that, for instance, exclude groups or facilitate privilege or support modes of thinking and operating that disadvantage particular groups in society. Lived theology, even when it is problematic or mistaken, will not simply be a set of doctrines or ideas; it will be woven into life and practice. It is a living cultural environment. This means that the theological task of understanding and then offering insight and correction that practical theology sets out to do is far from straightforward. Lived theology is charged with emotions and commitments, and making changes requires more than ideas alone. Practical theology, then, is the discipline that seeks to help churches as they strive to be faithful in the lived theological environment.

## Paying Attention to Lived Theology

In this chapter I have argued that practical theology is first and primarily the discipline of paying critical attention to lived theology. In the ongoing lives of communities, lived theology exists as the thread that runs through the multiple layers of expression from the formal and institutional voices to the more implicit and individual kinds of theology that are carried in actions and gesture. Practical theology has the task in the church of examining and expressing the dynamics and patterns that exist within lived theology. The purpose in paying attention to lived theology is first to understand; second, to draw attention to what is going on; and third, to help communities as they seek to alter patterns that might be unhelpful or problematic. All of these roles for practical theology necessitate a theory of how practice and theology interact in lived communities. My suggestion for this kind of theorizing has drawn on the three notions of lived religion, ordinary theology, and the four voices methodology. I concluded by setting out how these three theories can be combined as lived theology and how this can inform and shape the way we approach practical theology.

# 5

# Practical Theology as a Conversation about Practice and Theology

Practical theology has its origins and purpose in the local church, but it is also an academic discipline. At its heart this discipline is a conversation. This conversation is complex and multilayered, but essentially it is about one thing: method. The methodological issue that dominates practical theology is carried in its name. How is it possible to talk about theology and practice? "Theology" and "practice" have one thing in common. They are words that are difficult to pin down. As I have already suggested, theology can exist as different genres and operate in different voices, modes, and locations. Practice might, in contrast, appear to offer a more certain and concrete area for study. Unfortunately, this is not necessarily the case. Practice, as we have seen in the previous chapter, is related to the lived and hence to questions of culture, context, community, and identity.

In this chapter, the methodological issues that lie at the heart of the discipline of practical theology will be explored through a survey of key thinkers within the discipline. Each section will introduce the ideas of different practical theologians and how they have approached doing practical theology (i.e., how both practice and theology should be taken seriously).

The idea of conversation in the discipline of practical theology is used to indicate that there are really quite different approaches to these central issues within the discipline.

I divide this chapter into four sections: "Practical Theology as Ministerial Education," "Correlational Approaches to Practical Theology," "Practical Theology as Interpreting Action," and "A Return to Theology and Tradition." Each section conceives of practical theology in a different way. If you are new to the field, this can be quite confusing, but the key issue here is how practice and theology connect. What you need to ask as we explore these theories is, What approach to theology and practice do I find most helpful?

## Practical Theology as Ministerial Education

Practical theology as a theological discipline owes its origins to the education of ministers. As a result, reflection on the practice of leadership and the various roles and functions of clergy has been one of the most fruitful areas within the discipline. Traditionally, practical theology, as it deals with ministerial education, has been divided into different fields of study. These in turn have become rich areas for research and theological reflection in their own right. So theological discussion of preaching, for instance, has grown into the field of homiletics, teaching has developed as Christian education, and in recent years there has been the development of the field of youth ministry. The study of evangelism has given birth to the disciplinary area of mission studies. Mission studies has come almost full circle and is now at the center of conversations about the future shape of the church. Pastoral care has been one of the most significant areas within practical theology. The study of worship also has evolved its own separate disciplinary area known as liturgical studies. Added to these is the area of church organization and administration, which has become something of a boom area with fields such as congregational studies, church development, and church growth, not to mention the more applied aspects of ecclesiology.

So practical theology as ministerial education has generated an extraordinary range of writing and thinking. Perhaps as a result, reflection on the practice of ministry has led to creative and significant insights that have moved the discipline of practical theology in important ways. At the center of these have been methodological perspectives on how theology and practice relate to each other. In the next sections we will explore the contribution that ministerial education has made at a theoretical level through the writing of three practical theologians: Clement F. Rogers, who was a lecturer and then professor of pastoral theology at King's College, London (1906–32); Seward Hiltner, discussed briefly in chapter 1, who taught at Princeton Seminary (1961–80); and Craig Dykstra, who served as senior vice president for religion at the Lilly Endowment (1989–2012). Both Rogers and Hiltner talk about reflection on ministry as pastoral theology rather than as practical theology.

In the United Kingdom, the view of pastoral theology as relating to the discipline of educating for ministry has been quite common. In the United States, however, pastoral theology is typically thought of as describing theological approaches to pastoral care and counseling. These disparities about names are significant because they indicate the extent to which practical theology is an evolving and sometimes confusing conversation.

### Clement Rogers and the Science of Ministry

Published just before the outbreak of the First World War, *An Introduction to the Study of Pastoral Theology* offers a vision of what Rogers speaks of as a positive science of pastoral ministry. What he means by a science is the possibility that through a diligent and attentive engagement in the practice of ministry, clergy could begin to establish rules and principles for the effective operation of their calling. Rogers defines theology as the science of human relations with God. Practical theology is the area of theology that explores the social expression and mediation of these relationships.[1] The starting point for pastoral theology is the willingness to be fully engaged in the practice of ministry. As Rogers puts it, "We may begin in our own parishes and by hard, disciplined thought try to make our work effective, searching out by what spiritual laws the healing of souls may be furthered, so we may fight the powers of evil in heavenly places and not as those that beat in the air."[2]

Pastoral theology is a calling that requires involvement and action. It is a service of humanity and of the church. Ultimately, to do pastoral

---

1. C. Rogers, *Introduction*, 36.
2. Ibid., 34.

theology, says Rogers, is to be a priest.[3] He explores this priestly element in relation to the different subject areas within pastoral theology. The first area he calls "devotion," which deals with the range of ways in which humanity is drawn into a relationship with God—what Rogers calls the "underlying laws of worship and the inner life."[4] This includes the study of worship and liturgy, but it also involves ascetic theology and Christian art. Ascetic theology explores the spiritual disciplines of the individual. "Christian art" is Rogers's term for all of the different cultural expressions of faith.

The second area covers both the content of "Christian truth" and the means by which this is communicated. Communication includes the science of preaching (homiletics) and the science of education. Rogers groups these together with apologetics and mission studies under the term "evangelization."

The third area is practical duty. This covers ethics, canon law, the study of church polity, and "practical work," including the moral education and the philanthropic work of the parish. These three subject areas within pastoral theology relate explicitly to the role of the parish priest. Devotion is "connected with the work of a clergyman as Minister of the Eucharist. Evangelization gathers all of those areas that link to 'a clergyman's duties as Evangelical and Minister of the Word.' The area of Practical Duty is symbolized by the role of the clergy as Ministers of Baptism."[5]

Pastoral theology, Rogers argues, is a practical science. As such, it combines learning from theoretical sources and learning from participation in ministry. He champions the minister as a reflective practitioner—that is, someone who learns while doing. He points out that many of the principles and the rules that govern the science of ministerial practice are yet to be discovered, and he encourages his readers to go out into the parish and set about learning as they are doing. To this end, he suggests a range of simple research methods such as keeping a regular journal of pastoral encounters, asking questions of the congregation about their experience of the service and particularly of preaching, and, especially in the early years of ministry, taking time to visit neighboring churches in order to learn about the variety of ways in which worship takes place.

3. Ibid., 43–45.
4. Ibid., 214.
5. Ibid., 214–15.

Rogers also points out that the social scientific disciplines of psychology and sociology have much to teach the minister, and these should also be used to form theories of practice. Alongside knowledge gained from practice is that gained from the traditional theological disciplines of biblical studies, patristics, doctrinal study, and church history. Each of these has its own internal method and focus and should not be confused with pastoral theology. But "every theological question," says Rogers, "has its pastoral side."[6] Theological, moral, and ethical principles are developed through traditional theological study, and then comes the question of how these are to be worked out in practice in the church and wider society. This is the subject area of pastoral theology.

### Seward Hiltner and the Pastoral Perspective

We briefly discussed Seward Hiltner in chapter 1. Hiltner's *Preface to Pastoral Theology* was published in 1958 and has been widely recognized as one of the modern classics of practical theology. Pastoral theology, says Hiltner, is a formal branch of theology that arises from the study of "Christian shepherding." Shepherding comes from the word "pastor," and it describes the function of the minister, but it also includes the study of those functions.[7] At its heart, shepherding is a perspective. "The term 'perspective' enables us to think of the subject, or shepherd, as having and exercising an attitude or point of view or type of feeling that is basic to him [or her] and not just something tacked on."[8] So pastoral theology is the branch of theology that brings this perspective to bear on all the operations and functions of the church and the minister.

The purpose of Hiltner's study is to develop "conclusions of a theological order from reflection on these observations."[9] Shepherding is not the only perspective that arises from the practice of ministry. There are also the functions of teaching and communicating the faith, along with all the operations connected to the organization of the Christian community. These in turn, says Hiltner, have their distinct and separate perspectives.

Pastoral theology is an autonomous field of theological study that has its place alongside the other theological disciplines. It is distinctive, says

6. Ibid.
7. Hiltner, *Preface to Pastoral Theology*, 15–16.
8. Ibid., 18.
9. Ibid., 20.

Hiltner, because it is operation-centered or function-centered in contrast to biblical studies or systematic theology, for instance, which are "logic-centered" in their method. Logic-centered disciplines include questions that relate to practice, and their findings have practical implications, but operation-centered forms of study, such as pastoral theology, are distinctive because their findings and theories emerge out of reflection on events, acts, and practices from a particular perspective. Pastoral theology organizes knowledge into a system of thought, but it does so through the lens of its particular interests.[10]

Pastoral theology, Hiltner says, is "an operation-focused branch of theology which begins with theological questions and concludes with theological answers, in the interim examining all acts and operations of pastor and church to the degree that they involve the perspective of Christian shepherding."[11] This field of inquiry involves the study of practice, but it also requires the generation of theological perspectives from the Bible and other theological texts. So theological insight within the pastoral perspective moves both from theological texts and their application and from practice and experience toward theological expression. These two directions of flow are not oppositional; both contribute to pastoral theology.

### Craig Dykstra and the Ecclesial and Pastoral Imagination

In *For Life Abundant*, coauthored with Dorothy Bass and published in 2008, Craig Dykstra focuses on the practices that shape the minister and the congregation. He calls these practices ecclesial and pastoral imagination. Imagination describes the innate, habituated ways that ministers and communities live out the Christian faith. This kind of wisdom only emerges through years of practice.

Ecclesial imagination is a way of seeing and being that comes about as Christian people share together as a community in the knowledge of God and seek to live an "abundant life." What results is a kind of wisdom that shapes the lives of disciples. Abundant life is expressed in daily ways of seeing and being both inside and outside the church. Ecclesial imagination is a distinct way of looking that is different in content and in quality from the dominant culture that surrounds the church. People in churches,

10. Ibid., 20–21.
11. Ibid., 24.

Dykstra claims, have a way of speaking that is slightly different from the conventional forms of wisdom. They are open to one another, they invest in young people, and they tend to be more generous with their money.[12]

Pastoral imagination is fundamentally related to the imagination of the Christian community. Each gives rise to the other. The intelligence and insight carried collectively in churches inform and shape ministers. This learning takes place almost unwittingly as ministers and congregations live with each other. Pastoral imagination, says Dykstra, is similarly organic in its development. Pastoral imagination is developed and grows through the many activities of ministry done with faithfulness and with integrity.[13] "Every day pastors are immersed in a constant, and sometimes nearly chaotic, interplay of meaning-filled relationships and demands." The activities of ministers vary from preaching and teaching to dealing with the fabric of buildings. On top of this, they have to respond quickly to a range of complex and unpredictable pastoral situations as they arise. It is the unique combination of all of these different challenges that forges the intelligence and wisdom of the pastor. As Dykstra puts it, "Life lived long enough and fully enough in pastoral office gives rise to a way of seeing in depth and of creating new realities that is an indispensable gift to the church, to all who are members of it, and, indeed, to public life and to the world."[14]

Practical theology, says Dykstra, is a vital resource for both ecclesial and pastoral imagination. The purpose of practical theology and of theological education in general is to nurture, discipline, and provide resources to the church and the minister. Practical theology helps to shape the purposes and vision of the abundant life. This abundant life is the "telos," or end goal, of pastoral imagination.[15] Dykstra draws on Dorothy Bass's understanding of practical theology as shaped around three questions: "How can, and how do, our lives and our life together participate in a way of life that reflects the life of God, both when we are gathered as church and when we are dispersed into countless disparate circumstances? What is the shape of a contemporary way of life that truly is life-giving in and for the sake of the world? And how can the church

12. Dykstra, "Pastoral and Ecclesial Imagination," 57.
13. Ibid., 47.
14. Ibid., 50–51.
15. Ibid., 43.

foster such a way of life, for the good of all creation?"[16] These concerns
are intimately connected to ecclesial and pastoral imagination. They
are the motivating force for the people of God. The challenge for those
involved in practical theology is to stay closely enough connected to the
lived life of communities and of Christian ministers that the discipline
is able to continually act as a nurturing, envisioning, and corrective
influence in the practice of faith.

### Ministerial Education and Practical Theology

In its origins, practical theology is fundamentally related to the life of
the church. This connection means that the education of ministers and
also lay people in leadership continues to shape the discipline. Clement
Rogers and Seward Hiltner, although they are separated by two world
wars and by the historical, cultural, and ecclesial differences between the
United States and the United Kingdom, share a basic theological orientation. Both writers see ministerial practice as an organizing framework
for theology. There is a perspective that comes from being a pastor and a
priest. This perspective is so significant that it can be used to reconfigure
the other theological disciplines. So Hiltner and Rogers argue that it is
possible to do biblical studies, systematic theology, and church history
with different questions in mind.

In the last thirty years there has been a strong tendency within practical theology to reject what is known as "applied theology," which seeks
to apply theological concepts to practice. Practical theology, it is argued,
starts with practice rather than by working out a doctrinal or a biblical
"theory" that it then relates to life.

Rogers and Hiltner, coming from a much earlier time, offer an important corrective to this rejection of applied forms of theologizing. They
suggest that it is possible to work within the traditional disciplines to
develop theories and insights. In fact, it is necessary and desirable to do
this kind of work, but what makes it practical theology is the "perspective" that comes from being an active minister and believer in the life of
the church. In other words, although the student or the academic might
be thinking in fairly abstract or theoretical ways, the ecclesial perspective
is embodied in the person doing the study. What distinguishes this kind

16. Ibid., 60.

of work as practical theology is that it attempts to foreground the questions and issues that arise from the life of the church—what Dykstra calls pastoral and ecclesial imagination. Communities and individuals carry and nurture habituated ways of approaching practice and theology in the everyday. This attention to practice moves the methodological discussion in practical theology from a relationship between subject areas in an academic discipline to the embodied life of communities.

There is one further and most significant contribution that these three writers illustrate. All three in their different ways are advocates of the use of empirical methods to study practice. Craig Dykstra, for instance, argues for the need to pay detailed attention to how imagination is embedded in practice. Clement Rogers sees empirical research as a way to discover the workings of God in the world. Seward Hiltner talks about the need to pay attention to the life of the church. In particular, his concept of a pastoral perspective arises from his involvement in developing ways of paying attention to the particularity of pastoral encounters that were characteristic of training in pastoral care and counseling in the United States for more than thirty years.

This turn toward empirical forms of knowledge has been a key characteristic of practical theology, but it has not been without its problems. Chief among these is the question of how theological forms of knowledge relate to methods and theoretical insights that have their origins in the social sciences. Academic forms of practical theology have been shaped in many ways by a conversation around how the social sciences and theology might be correlated. The correlation of different disciplines has been right at the heart of the conversation about method within practical theology.

## Correlational Approaches to Practical Theology

Correlation has had a deep and an enduring influence on the development of practical theology. The method is most closely associated with theologian Paul Tillich. Correlation for Tillich is the process whereby theological attention is paid to the questions that emerge from human cultural expression. These questions give rise to theological answers that draw upon the richness of the Christian tradition and divine revelation. This relationship of questioning and answering gives rise to a circle of communication. So the "divine-human" relationship is a correlation where "theology formulates the questions implied in human existence, and theology formulates the answer implied in divine self-manifestation under the guidance of the questions implied in human existence."[17]

### David Tracy and a Revised Correlational Method

The idea that theology was structured around a correlation between human questions and a divine answer was taken up and then significantly developed by David Tracy. Tracy embraced the notion that there were two sources for theological thinking. He calls these the "situation" and the "message." Where he and Tillich differ is in Tillich's assertion that the situation must be limited to asking questions for which the answers always come from the other source. This is unsatisfactory for Tracy, and so he offers what he calls a "revised correlational method" where not just the questions from human experience are considered but also the various answers that arise from that situation. The answers are then considered alongside those that come from "the message."[18]

Correlation for Tracy is linked directly to his understanding of practical theology as the ethical outworking of faith. In *The Analogical Imagination*, Tracy divides theology into three subdisciplines: fundamental theology, systematic theology, and practical theology. These subdisciplines are distinctive in their modes of inquiry, how they understand truth claims, their distinct requirements for faith commitment on behalf of the theologian, and, most significantly, their primary reference group or public.

All theology is public in one way or another, says Tracy, but practical theology has a particular role in this regard. While fundamental theology is primarily oriented toward the public world of the university and systematic to the church, practical theology expresses the engagement of theology with the wider society. It is particularly concerned with the religious significance of social and political movements, as well as developments in culture and in pastoral situations. As it gets taken up in these movements, practical theology becomes oriented around praxis rather than theoretical frameworks. It is this involvement with action that orients the practical theologian toward ethics. "Practical theologies will be concerned principally

17. Tillich, *Systematic Theology*, 61.
18. Tracy, *Blessed Rage*, 46.

with the ethical stance of responsible commitment to and sometimes even involvement in a situation of praxis."[19]

### Don Browning and a Fundamental Practical Theology

Don Browning was one of the most significant practical theologians in recent times. He taught in Chicago, where he was a longtime colleague of David Tracy. In *A Fundamental Practical Theology*, Browning develops a complex theory of theological method drawing heavily on Tracy's understanding of correlation and of practical theology as praxis. He takes as his starting point the ways in which Christian communities are places where practical reason is embodied in communal life. Through practice and through the various forms of symbolic communication, Christian communities carry within them resources for practical reason.

Practical theology is concerned first to understand and describe these aspects of the ethical life of the church and then to offer critical and corrective frameworks to help communities change and renew their praxis. The ethical focus of practical theology is expressed through two questions, says Browning: What shall we do? And how shall we live?[20] With this starting orientation toward the ethical life of the church, he develops his theory of a fundamental practical theology through four movements or tasks: the descriptive movement, the historical movement, the systematic movement, and strategic practical theology.

The descriptive movement centers on the task of interpreting and describing a situation. Browning sees this as a kind of hermeneutic sociology. "Practical theology describes practices in order to discern the conflicting cultural and religious meanings that guide our action and provoke the questions that animate our practical thinking."[21] A number of questions characterize this movement. These include: What are we doing? What symbols, ideals, and reasons do we use to interpret what we are doing? What are the sources and authorities for what we are doing, and what should we be doing? This last question leads directly into the next task, which Browning calls the historical movement. In this movement, there is a turn toward the texts and the traditional disciplines of

19. Tracy, *Analogical Imagination*, 57.
20. Browning, *Fundamental Practical Theology*, 10.
21. Ibid., 48.

theology—that is, biblical studies, church history, and the history of Christian thought. These theological disciplines, with their different approaches to criticism and knowledge, are used as a "distancing" technique in the service of understanding praxis. As such they are positioned by Browning within an overarching theological method of fundamental practical theology.

The next task brings the different areas of knowledge together. This is the systematic movement. What takes place is a fusion of "the vision implicit in contemporary practices and the vision implied in the practices of the normative texts."[22] Systematic theology sets out to develop an ordered and arranged view of the various sources—both those from praxis and those from traditional theological texts. Its overall aim is to bring together the general themes from the gospel with the questions that emerge from and characterize the situations in the present moment.

The final task is what Browning calls strategic practical theology. This movement is shaped around four basic questions: (1) How do we understand this concrete situation in which we must act? To address this question, it is required that we have examined individual and corporate histories, including specific commitments that shape action and the systems that support communities and individuals in their praxis. (2) What should be our praxis in this concrete situation? This brings together the results from the first three movements, and it starts to engage specifically with the norms that arise from the review of texts in the historical and systematic movements. (3) How do we critically defend the norms and therefore our praxis in this concrete situation? This involves developing an apologetic for the practice of the community. (4) What means, strategies, and rhetoric should we use in this concrete situation? This involves developing specific plans for the church to engage in praxis.

### Stephen Pattison and Words That Resurrect the Dead

Browning's fundamental practical theology uses correlation, but it structures this within a pattern of analysis from the pastoral cycle. The pastoral cycle will be discussed in depth in the next chapter. At this point, it is important simply to note how Browning's method and others like it generate a method for practical theology that is structured around specific

22. Ibid., 51.

moves or stages. Each has its ordered place. To follow the method is to transition through these stages.

One of the problems with this approach is that it tends to insulate each of the areas of interest from the others. You have to pass through the one to get to the other. In practice, however, things are always more organic, slightly messy, and mixed up together. So for instance, it is almost impossible to turn off our knowledge of theological texts and the traditions of the church or the material in the Bible as we examine the practice of the church. Indeed, as Browning says, praxis is itself a form of theology in action or a "theory-laden practice."[23] So the correlation method is probably better understood in more organic and dynamic ways. This is precisely what the British practical theologian Stephen Pattison explores in his approach to correlation.[24]

Pattison comes to practical theology from a background of working with those who are in psychiatric care. In 1981 he published *A Critique of Pastoral Care*. The book was a groundbreaking work in practical theology, giving an in-depth critical analysis of the various secularizing tendencies in the prevailing approaches to counseling and pastoral care. His background in mental health and the world of the hospital and chaplaincy informs Pattison's understanding of pastoral theology and the way that correlation works in practice.[25] He defines pastoral theology as "a place where religious belief, tradition and practice meets contemporary experiences, questions and actions and conducts a dialogue which is mutually enriching, intellectually critical and practically transforming."[26]

Pattison argues for pastoral theology as a vivid, dancing, and puzzling practice. It is a vibrant practice that should by rights find a place at the heart of the church and in the world beyond. Indeed, pastoral theology is precisely the place where the theology and the faith of the church come into contact with the thoughts, ideas, and practices of the wider world. What takes place at the point of meeting is a conversation, a dialogue that is designed to bring about insight, critical comment, and transformation. This is a visionary or prophetic enterprise. As Pattison says, "In practicing pastoral theology I look for words that raise the dead, that fundamentally

23. Ibid., 6.
24. Pattison, *Critique of Pastoral Care*.
25. Pattison, *Challenge of Practical Theology*, 12–21.
26. Pattison, *Critique of Pastoral Care*, 227.

change perceptions, that transform people, society and the world because of their symbolic power; words that make a difference."[27] In biblical theology, the words of God are themselves acts and deeds. In speech, God brings about events and enacts God's will.

Dialogue is fundamentally correlational, but it is not constructed as a particular method. Pattison resists the development of an abstract series of tasks or moves. Rather, he locates dialogue in the context of practice. For pastoral workers, there is a daily necessity to make sense of what they are doing. Faced with the range of articulate and convincing frameworks for action that secular professionals advocate in the arena of pastoral care, an adequate theology is a necessity. A plausible and communicable explanation of why and how Christians can engage in shared practice alongside others is a necessity. It is fundamentally about the identity of the pastoral workers as Christians in the public sphere. This expression of identity, however, will itself be, to some extent, informed by other practitioners. There is a dialogue that takes place between practitioners and the various theoretical frameworks that inform their practice. Dialogue involves mutual learning in public spaces. "By developing articulate pastoral theology, people are in principle in a much better position to explain themselves to a variety of audiences."[28] It is conversation that lies at the heart of these kinds of encounters, says Pattison.

Conversation should be both critical and creative. At the most basic level, it involves a three-way dialogue between (1) our own ideas, beliefs, feelings, and assumptions; (2) the ideas, beliefs, feelings, and assumptions of the wider Christian community; and (3) the individuals, communities, ideas, feelings, and assumptions that are present in the situation that we are engaging with.[29] Pattison sees conversation as a flexible and fluid form of theologizing. It can be formal, but more often it is informal. Conversations do not always lead to conclusions or even to defined ways of acting. They are simply a way in which life is enriched and sociality maintained. For Pattison, pastoral theology is like a lake that is complex, rich, and flowing and that can be seen in different ways and made use of for different purposes. Correlation therefore shifts from method toward an organic element in the lived practice of faith both inside and outside the Christian community.

27. Ibid., 221.
28. Ibid., 224.
29. Ibid., 230.

## Practical Theology as Interpreting Action

In recent years practical theology has seen a significant shift toward understanding itself as the interpretation of action. In the 1970s, German theologian Norbert Mette set out this approach to the discipline. Practical theology, says Mette, "must be conceived of as a theological theory of action within a theology that is understood as a practice-orientated science."[30] This understanding of practical theology locates it within theology but derives its orientation to its area of study ultimately from the social sciences. Central to this approach is a shift away from theology defined as talk about God toward practical theology as the discussion of how communities, through their practices, express their understanding of God. Theology thereby becomes a kind of cultural or sociological study. This theoretical move within the discipline can be illustrated by the work of two practical theologians: Gerben Heitink and Elaine Graham.

### Gerben Heitink and Theology Mediated in Praxis

In *Practical Theology: History, Theory, Action, and Domains*, Dutch practical theologian Gerben Heitink sets out a complex theory of practical theology as a theory of action. He defines the discipline as "the empirically orientated theological theory of the mediation of the Christian faith in the praxis of modern society."[31] For Heitink, a decisive shift toward anthropology is involved in this theoretical understanding. This move, he argues, has its origins in the work of German theologian Friedrich Schleiermacher. It is characterized by a shift away from understanding theology as the rational discussion or science of the being and nature of God toward the study of the human experience of God and the Christian faith as a cultural form. Revelation, Heitink argues, is only perceived through human experience. We study humanity rather than divinity or, more correctly, divinity as it is seen in and through human action. Faith itself rather than God becomes the object of study. For Heitink, "Faith is the direct object of theology. God, the indirect object, cannot be the topic of inquiry. God is only the direct object of our faith."[32]

---

30. Mette, *Theorie der Praxis*, 9, quoted in Heitink, *Practical Theology*, 102.
31. Heitink, *Practical Theology*, 102.
32. Ibid., 111.

The central task of practical theology is to formulate a "practical-theological theory." This involves developing a theological understanding of action. Action, says Heitink, is essentially communicative. Actions convey meaning. They are therefore open to be interpreted and read as texts. In the ecclesial context, action exists within the theological framework of the kingdom of God. "It is directed toward the 'already' and the 'not yet' of God's kingdom, in the dialectic of anamnesis and anticipation, of remembering and expecting."[33]

Heitink sees practical theology as the science of the interpretation of the action of the church. Within this framework, he argues that all practical theological questions revolve around a hermeneutical, an empirical, and a strategic perspective. Strategic issues connect to a variety of fields or domains of action. He describes these as operating on three levels. "Micro" questions concern the individual, "meso" questions concern the functioning of groups, and questions that relate to the wider society make up the "macro" level.[34] The hermeneutical perspective orients the study toward questions such as "who does what?" and most importantly "why?" So the inquiry moves toward an examination of intentions and an understanding of the motivations that lie behind actions. Understanding action involves an investigation into the reasons why people and communities act in certain ways. The empirical perspective connects the "who does what" with the "where and when" questions that relate to action. This in turn involves the use of a range of different research methods drawn from the social sciences to help in the understanding of a situation.[35]

### Elaine Graham and Transforming Practice

Elaine Graham is one of the leading practical theologians in the United Kingdom. Her book *Transforming Practice* has become a core text in contemporary understanding of the discipline. Pastoral theology, she argues, "is critical phenomenology, studying a living and acting faith-community in order to excavate and examine the norms which inhabit pastoral praxis." There should be no appeal to theological sources that exist beyond the life of the church; rather, the role of the theologian is to explore and articulate

33. Ibid., 155.
34. Ibid., 214.
35. Ibid., 220–40.

the ways in which communities "order their life" through theologically informed practice and principles.[36]

Communities carry in their practices theological norms and values. So theology is always studied as it is embodied in concrete practices in communal life. Graham reads practice through the notion of "situated knowledge," which she derives from feminist writer Donna Haraway. Haraway sees knowledge and identity as provisional and changeable constructs, but these have an ethical and moral dimension because they are expressed through embodiment and relationship and in concrete situations (TP, 9).

This situated understanding of knowledge leads Graham to challenge the notion that there is any kind of transcendent system of thought available to the theologian or the church that exists beyond practice. "Effectively, gender challenges pastoral practice to refuse any system of sources and norms which lies in metaphysics or beyond human agency or mediation" (TP, 141). This is not to say that Christian communities do not have any norms or values but that these do not exist apart from the practices and the lived expression of faith.

The life of the church should not be equated with the "acting out" of predetermined moral frameworks or of doctrinal formulations (TP, 11). Rather, the study of religion should focus on the ways in which communities construct particular cultural forms of life and expression. These cultural forms shape themselves and structure reality in subcultural ways that operate as sources of social relationship for groups as well as for individuals. These social constructs carry theological understanding. They mediate the divine in human cultural forms. Pastoral practices are thus the "expression of the Christian presence in the world," and they should be seen as the "foundation" rather than as the application of theological understanding (TP, 111).

Questions of normativity and of authority are not to be seen as being located outside community life and expression, but they are articulated and carried within practice. Theological norms are enacted, says Graham, and embodied in praxis. The community "inhabits" truth claims, and these generate "moral ways of life, story-telling, promoting human development and pursuing gender equality" (TP, 139).

36. Graham, *Transforming Practice*, 140 (hereafter cited in text as *TP*).

For Graham, theological understanding is embedded within practice and communal life. The theologian articulates the theological frameworks that are carried in practice and the lived. So for Graham, pastoral theology is primarily a form of interpretation that focuses on the social and cultural reality of the Christian community. Through paying attention to the embodied expression of groups and individuals, an idea of transcendence is developed. Thus, alongside interpretation, the pastoral theologian is able to contribute to the ongoing life of the church by being able to articulate theological frameworks and norms as they are embedded within practices (*TP*, 140). "My vision of pastoral theology," says Graham, "portrays it as the systematic reflection upon the nature of the church in the world, accessible only through the practical wisdom of those very communities." Pastoral theology does not operate in a "legislative way" in relation to practice; rather, it works to help the community of faith to find a "critical and public account of its purposeful presence in the world and the values that give shape to its actions." This means that pastoral theology operates with and alongside communities as they seek to be transformative of society and their own ecclesial life through an ongoing, self-aware, and self-critical praxis (*TP*, 208–10).

## A Return to Theology and Tradition

Alongside the dominant methodological approaches of correlation and hermeneutics has been what might be called a "theological" approach to practical theology. Proponents of this sort of methodological contribution have tended to position it as a corrective to what they see as the erosion of more traditional theological ways of thinking about practice. To illustrate these voices in the conversation around method, I'll introduce two American practical theologians, Thomas Oden and Ray Anderson.

### Thomas Oden and Rediscovering the Classic Tradition

Written in 1984, Thomas Oden's *Care of Souls in the Classic Tradition* is an impassioned plea for a change in direction in practical theology. Oden frames his argument with a personal narrative. He explains that, influenced by the work of Seward Hiltner and prevailing trends in the United States, he had for many years sought to understand pastoral care through a dialogue with psychological theory and the field of professional counseling. After several years of working within these disciplinary fields, he found himself questioning the extent to which the Christian church had lost something fundamental to itself by embracing what were largely secular theories of the self and of therapy.

Oden explores what he calls the classic tradition of pastoral care, arguing that before modern psychological theories, the church had developed its own ways of thinking about pastoral care. This tradition, he says, is in the Pastoral Epistles of the New Testament. It is also in the patristic writings of Cyprian, Tertullian, John Chrysostom, and Ambrose. It is found in medieval writers Hugh of Saint Victor and Thomas Aquinas. It is present at the Reformation in the work of Martin Luther, John Calvin, and Ulrich Zwingli and then in the reflections of Anglican and Puritan thinkers such as George Herbert and Richard Baxter.[37] For Oden, although this is a varied and exclusively male list, it represents a single and developing tradition. This tradition, he argues, is "unified by its Eucharistic center and its concern to embody the living Christ through interpersonal meeting."[38]

Oden argues that the classic tradition of pastoral care has been all but abandoned in practical theology. To illustrate this assertion, he conducted a review of the texts on pastoral care and counseling, first from the seven most-read authors of the latter part of the nineteenth century and then from seven writers from the twentieth century. Oden found a marked difference. In the nineteenth-century writings, reference was made quite frequently to texts and sources from the classic tradition. In the twentieth-century writings, which included Seward Hiltner, Howard Clinebell, and Paul Tournier, he found not a single reference to earlier Christian writings on pastoral care.

With this insight, Oden then surveyed the twentieth-century writers on pastoral care for the number of occasions they referenced contemporary psychotherapists such as Sigmund Freud, Carl Jung, or Carl Rogers. He found that every one of the contemporary works on pastoral theology cited secular psychotherapists with considerable frequency.[39] Oden says that this is clear evidence of the erosion of the classic theological approaches

37. Oden, *Care of Souls*, 27.
38. Ibid., 28.
39. Ibid., 29–31.

to pastoral care within the Christian church. At the start of the twentieth century, a sea change took place. "During these decades," he says, "we have witnessed wave after wave of various hegemonies of emergent psychologies being accommodated, often cheaply, into pastoral care without much self-conscious identity formation from the tradition."[40]

The accommodation of psychological theory has meant that Christian approaches to pastoral care have become all but indistinguishable from secular counterparts. There has been a collective and at times a willful forgetfulness of the classic tradition. In many cases, the psychological theories adopted are themselves opposed to traditional Christian understandings of the self. Yet even where more polemical positions have been avoided, Christian pastoral care has suffered from the loss of its rich heritage. Most significantly, this loss has resulted in an inability to reason theologically about pastoral practice.

Oden argues that there is therefore an urgent need for those working in pastoral care to rediscover the theological voices from the past. It is no longer acceptable, he says, for Christian practice to be defined by psychology. The task to be done is to define the field in theological terms. Basic to this project is the need for paying close attention to those premodern authors who constitute the classic tradition of pastoral care. "We must define for ourselves again what pastoral care is and in what sense pastoral theology is and remains theology."[41]

This turn to theology, however, does not mean that Oden entirely rejects contemporary psychological theory or psychotherapeutic professional practice. Neither does he advocate an uncritical return to premodern ways of thinking. He simply wants to see pastoral theology recover its sense of self in relation to secularizing forces, and to do this it needs to begin to draw upon the wealth of the Christian theological tradition.[42]

### Ray Anderson and Practical Theology as Christopraxis

In *The Shape of Practical Theology*, published in 2001, Ray Anderson sets out to offer a theological framework for practical theology. Practical theology, he argues, is a "critical engagement with the interface between

40. Ibid., 32.
41. Ibid.
42. Ibid.

the word of God as revealed through Scripture and the work of God taking place in and through the church in the world."[43] Theology for Anderson is deeply and intrinsically practical. It is not necessary, he argues, to find artificial methodological constructs to connect theology to practice. Theology is practical because of Christ. "What makes theology practical is not the fitting of orthopedic devices to theoretical concepts in order to make them walk. Rather, theology occurs as a divine partner joins us in our walk, stimulating our reflection and inspiring us to recognize the living word as it happened to the two walking on the road to Emmaus on the first Easter."[44] The presence of Christ makes our theology a living theology.[45]

Anderson sees practical theology in christological terms. His term for this is "Christopraxis." Christopraxis is "the continuing ministry of Christ through the power and presence of the Holy Spirit."[46] This emphasis on Christ means that practical theology is both ecclesial and missional in focus. Mission, says Anderson, precedes the church. It is the praxis of God in and through the Holy Spirit; resulting from this mission, the church emerges as a sign of the kingdom of God in the world.[47] Mission theology, he says, must be an integral part of practical theology.[48]

With this distinctive theological starting point and orientation, Anderson then engages with the framework for practical theology as it is described by Don Browning. He agrees with Browning that at its heart practical theology is an exercise in understanding and interpreting the practice of the church. But for Anderson this praxis is seen not in ethical terms but through the lens of Christology. Practical theological method is shaped around stages similar to those described by Browning. This starts with the stage of interpretation and then moves to understanding and theological reflection, which leads to developing revised normative ways of acting.

But this whole process, Anderson argues, is profoundly theological. Theological reflection has its origins in the "context and crisis" of ministry. Present-day practice, however, is seen as the work of the risen Christ

---

43. Anderson, *Shape of Practical Theology*, 8.
44. Ibid., 12.
45. Ibid., 23–24, drawing on Torrance, *Reality and Evangelical Theology*, 138.
46. Anderson, *Shape of Practical Theology*, 29.
47. Ibid., 30.
48. Ibid., 31.

through the power of the Spirit. In attempting to correct and inform this praxis, it is necessary to draw upon Scripture. The interpretation of Scripture in turn is also the work of Christ though the Holy Spirit in the church. So both present-day practice and practical theology as an interpretative and normative discipline are christologically oriented and conditioned. Theological reflection, says Anderson, is "the activity of the Christian and the church by which acts of ministry are critically and continually assessed in the light of both revelation and reconciliation of God's true word." This truth, however, cannot be separated from personal faith, and personal faith in turn cannot be detached from the truth of God's being and Word.[49]

### Evaluating Theories and Themes

This chapter has introduced a number of key thinkers in practical theology. They represent what can be a rather bewildering range of ways of thinking about theology and practice. Part of the task we have in working within practical theology is to understand and then evaluate different approaches. I should probably say I don't agree with many of these writers, but even those I disagree with often have things that can help me. If you are starting out in practical theology, a key task is to map the field and then locate your own preferred approach within it. To help you with this, I want to identify a number of key themes around the relationship between theology and practice that emerge from the diverse range of practical theological writing presented in this chapter.

At the beginning of the twentieth century, practical theologians who were engaged in the education of clergy began to introduce new ways of talking about practice. For Clement Rogers, the practice of clergy and of the church was open to examination. He introduced his students to forms of observation and recording that could inform their practice. Seward Hiltner, writing in the United States forty years later, was also an advocate of a disciplined attention to practice that made use of forms of research that were informed by the social sciences.

This turn toward the social sciences gave rise to exciting and innovative ways of doing practical theology, but it also raised significant

49. Ibid., 55.

methodological issues. Chief among these was the question of how traditional forms of theological thought and knowledge were to relate to practice as it is described and theorized through empirical study. For Rogers and Hiltner, knowledge of pastoral practice develops an orientation or a perspective that gives theological study a particular purpose and direction. This in and of itself was helpful, but it left largely unexplored the question of how a specifically theological form of knowledge, even one that has been oriented toward practice, should be related to social scientific knowledge.

The relationship between social scientific and theological ways of describing and knowing lies right at the heart of correlational theory. Don Browning takes David Tracy's idea of critical correlation and locates it as a central move in practical theology. Correlation delineates a specific stage in practical theology for the church and its practices to be described using social scientific methods of inquiry. Theology similarly is allocated a stage in the way that practical theology addresses issues in the life of the church. The final stage, what Browning calls a strategic practical theology, arises from bringing together, through correlation, social scientific and theological forms of knowledge.

Browning's work has been deeply influential in practical theology, and for many practical theologians correlation has been, to steal a phrase from Browning, "fundamental." Stephen Pattison's dialogical approach shows how, for many ministerial practitioners working, for instance, as chaplains in hospitals or as youth workers, correlation is basically a way of life. This is quite simply because ministers who work outside a church setting must find ways to dialogue with colleagues who bring different professional and theoretical ways of thinking into the work setting. Here the idea of dialogue and mutual enrichment is not only helpful; it is essential.

Correlation has for some time been the dominant method in practical theology. Dominant ways of thinking, however, inevitably attract some criticism. One form of criticism comes from ideas of interpretation. Hermeneutical approaches tend to critique the way theology operates in the correlational method. For Heitink and for Graham, theology is something that should be understood as part of the cultural expression of the church, and as a result, theology should not be situated as an independent and distinctive voice. Theology is always embodied and has a place in the life of the community. So if it has an authority or a discriminating purpose, this comes from its situation within practices. One result of this move is that theology has no authority in and of itself; it only has this as it is so regarded by particular communities.

This move within practical theology is highly significant. It represents a kind of victory for practice over theology. Practice and how it is understood—that is, through social scientific and empirical methods—appears to have swallowed up theology as a distinct enterprise. It is interesting at this point to consider Craig Dykstra's discussion of the role of practical theology in ecclesial and pastoral imagination. Practical theology, he says, informs, nurtures, and critiques habituated forms of practice. In other words, there is a crucial role for some kind of evaluative assessment and creative envisioning in practical theology. This is very close to the different ways that Rowan Williams talks about theology as being at times celebration, communication, and also critique. The question remains, What are the resources for developing a renewed and refreshed vision of the church, particularly if theology is seen primarily as something located within a community's life?

For Thomas Oden, a return to theological forms of thinking and knowing is an urgent necessity. In a situation in which a distinctively Christian approach to pastoral care has been eroded, the classic tradition represents a corrective voice from outside. Of course, the interesting thing is that from a theological point of view, the church as a community does not simply consist of those who are in church now but also includes those who have gone before and indeed those who are yet to be part of the church. So these texts and various writings are simply the voices of this wider historical community.

For Ray Anderson, however, theological reflection is not simply a distinctive form of cultural communication. Theology and action are a work of Christ by the power of the Holy Spirit. This insight introduces a key issue in practical theology: God. For ordinary Christians and churches, talk about God and experiencing God's presence, power, and grace belong together. Talk about God is never an academic exercise. This kind of commonsense aphorism has a significant truth because it is the location of talk about God in an academic context that dislocates theology from the life of the church. On the face of it, hermeneutical approaches to practical theology seem to address this issue by situating theology as part of communal life.

The drawback with this is that it does not take account of the ways in which talk about God within a church context always holds within it the possibility of the transcendent—the occasions where friends are walking together, as Anderson says, and Christ comes alongside and the familiar is turned upside down.

# 6

# Theological Reflection

The everyday flow of church life takes place with very little mention of practical theology, let alone the theories that have been discussed in the previous chapter. As a result, despite the fact that churches are all the time thinking about faith and practice, most Christians have very little awareness that something called practical theology actually exists, unless they sign up for some kind of formal theological education. In the classroom setting, the most common way of teaching practical theology is to reflect theologically on practice. In some kinds of training for ministry, particularly among clergy in training, theological reflection is a requirement. Wherever formal practice placements are built in to the academic expectations, there will certainly be theological reflection.

The idea of reflection is overwhelmingly positive. At its most basic, it reinforces the vitally important perception that theology is not just something that other people have written about in books; everyone should and can think theologically about practice. Theological reflection is in many ways where the rubber hits the road. It is the place where we move from reading what other people have said and critiquing the theories in the textbooks to doing this thing called practical theology.

Doing practical theology can take a great many forms. It might be a report on a visit to a church for a class. It could be a regular meeting with a learning group to reflect theologically on what is being learned during training. We can reflect theologically by talking in groups, but there may also be occasions where written assignments are set. Theological reflection can be written up in a short report, or it may be a much more lengthy dissertation or doctoral thesis. Whatever the specific format, theological reflection represents a methodological challenge. Put quite simply, how do we think about practice theologically in a way that sheds light on and then makes a difference to the ongoing life of the church?

Given the range of methodological and theoretical debates in practical theology, it is quite surprising that when it comes to theological reflection as part of the curriculum, there is really only one method that is often taught: the pastoral cycle. This chapter starts, then, by discussing the pastoral cycle, but it then presents several examples of practical theology that offer different ways to think theologically about practice.

## The Pastoral Cycle

The pastoral cycle is so common in the teaching of practical theology that it has in many ways come to define the whole field. There are innumerable versions of the cycle, but they all try to structure how a practitioner thinks through a pastoral situation by offering a series of stages that shape the reflection. It is called a cycle because the process of reflection is meant to start with and then inform and even transform a particular situation or an incident.

The origins of the pastoral cycle are relatively recent. In 1912 Cardinal Joseph Cardijn started the Young Christian Workers in Belgium. Cardijn taught the workers to look beyond the surface for theological and social issues when they started to minister in industrial and workplace settings. He developed a formula that they should follow: see, judge, act. Seeing involves a thorough review of a concrete situation. What emerges from this review is then assessed, or brought to judgment, through the principles of Catholic teaching, and as a result, a plan for action is developed.

Cardijn's approach to theological reflection has been deeply influential in the Roman Catholic Church. In 1961 Pope John XXII formally endorsed the method as being significant for Catholic pastoral theology.[1] As liberation theology began to develop, Cardijn's see-judge-act method for theological reflection was given a more theoretical grounding through the work of Brazilian educationalist Paulo Freire. In *The Pedagogy of the*

1. *Mater et Magistra* 236.

*Oppressed*, Freire developed a theory of "conscientization" in which those who were poor and oppressed in communities, through a process of reflection, can gain perspectives that may lead to liberative action. People are rooted in situations, says Freire, and "they will tend to reflect on their own situationality to the extent that it challenges them to act upon it. People *are* because they *are* in a situation. And *they will be more* the more they not only critically reflect upon their existence but critically act upon it." Heavily influenced by Marxism, Freire sees reflection as an examination of the "very condition of existence."[2] By this he means the material circumstances and relations in which the poor and the oppressed find themselves.

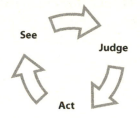

Through Freire, the pastoral cycle became a foundational method within liberation theology. So, for instance, the liberation theologian Gustavo Gutiérrez sees reflection as a fundamental part of liberation. It is the means by which the poor become aware of themselves and of their situation, and in this they discover their own language. Through a continual process of reflection, they are able to throw off "oppressive consciousness" and dependency and thereby find ways to engage in "transformation and the building up of society."[3]

Alongside its development in liberation theology and in the Roman Catholic Church, the pastoral cycle has also been made popular through the educational thinking of Daniel Kolb. In the 1980s Kolb argued that people do not learn from experience alone. They need to go through a process of reflection and conceptualization before they are able to develop ways to transform their practice. To facilitate this he developed a model for experiential learning. The model takes the form of a cycle that encourages a continual reflective engagement with experience. The Kolb learning cycle has four stages: (1) concrete experience—doing and

2. Freire, *Pedagogy of the Oppressed*, 80–81.
3. Gutiérrez, *Theology of Liberation*, 91–92.

having experiences; (2) reflective observation—the process of reviewing and reflecting on experience; (3) abstract conceptualization—concluding and learning from experience; and (4) active experimentation.[4]

In practical theology, the pastoral cycle has been developed in a variety of ways. A good summary of different models of the pastoral cycle can be found in Judith Thompson's excellent study guide *Theological Reflection*. Examples of slightly different forms of the cycle with different stages are found in the work of Paul Ballard and John Pritchard, Richard Osmer, and Johannes van der Ven.

In *Practical Theology in Action*, Paul Ballard and John Pritchard set out their version of the cycle. The starting point in the process of reflection is the everyday context of experience. Here the prompt for reflection is the experience of an interruption or a tension. This interruption sets off the need for exploration. This is a stage in which the situation is subjected to analysis in order to understand what is taking place. Exploration then leads on to reflection. Reflection is a process in which a variety of different forms of knowledge and of knowing are brought to bear on the situation, including the theological resources of the Christian faith. The final stage is action. Growing out of the two stages that precede it, a plan for a new approach to a pastoral situation is developed. Action then completes the cycle because it takes the reflection into the field of experience and practice.[5]

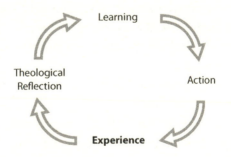

American practical theologian Richard Osmer has developed a model for theological reflection based on the pastoral cycle. His model is shaped around what he calls "the four tasks of practical theological interpretation."[6]

---

4. Kolb, *Experiential Learning*.
5. Ballard and Pritchard, *Practical Theology in Action*, 77–78.
6. Osmer, *Practical Theology*, 11. Osmer enumerates the four tasks, discussed below, throughout the book.

These tasks provide a structured sequence designed to help ministers explore issues in their practice. Each task is linked to a series of questions that connect the method to the everyday practices of the minister.

Osmer's starting point is the question, what is going on? He is imagining that, in the context of the practice of ministry, situations arise that are puzzling and complex. The experience of confusion in the context of practice prompts the first stage in the cycle, what Osmer calls the first task of practical theology: the descriptive-empirical task. This is characterized by a process of gathering information about what has taken place in an attempt to uncover patterns and relationships within a particular event. The actual situation or event might be, for example, a conflict in a church community or a problem in an individual's life. Gathering information may take the form of informal conversations, but it might also involve more formal methods of study and inquiry.

The next question, why is this going on? arises from the information that has been gathered. This leads into the next task: the interpretative task. Here different theories are explored to see if they can give a new perspective on the situation, and various insights from academic study are examined in the expectation that they might shed light and help in the development of insights on the pastoral situation.

In light of these various forms of knowledge, Osmer introduces the question of theological norms with the next question, what should be going on? This leads to the third task in practical theology: the normative task. Here theological concepts are introduced to help in the interpretation of particular situations and episodes in order to develop ethical norms that can guide "good practice."

All of these tasks lead up to the crucial question, how might we respond? and the final stage: the pragmatic task. This final stage involves the creation of specific pastoral strategies that grow out of the preceding stages and seek to make a difference in the original pastoral situation.

One of the most influential figures in the development of practical theology is Dutch scholar Johannes van der Ven. Van der Ven frames practical theology around a particular empirical methodology, which he calls "empirical theology." This method is structured in a series of moves: "the empirical-theological cycle." The starting point for the cycle is the development of a problem and a goal for the research. The method centers on identifying a particular problematic within the interpretative and communicative practice of the church. The cycle explores this problem through quantitative empirical means. But the method also sees the interpretative and communicative practices of the church as the goal of the research. So empirical theology has as its end goal to "improve" interpretative and communicative praxis or to free it from "constraints and expand its boundaries."[7]

Stage 2 van der Ven calls theological induction. This involves a dynamic interaction between perception of a particular issue and theological reflection. Reflection requires a survey of the key theological literature and also the empirical literature that relates to the designated problem. This leads to the framing of the theological question that shapes the direction of the research. Stage 3, theological deduction, involves developing theological concepts that will be used in stage 4: theological operationalization. In this stage, specific concepts are structured into testable or scalable formulations that can be used in the research process. This is usually achieved through a questionnaire. Stage 5, empirical-theological testing, involves data gathering. This is followed by stage 6, which is empirical-theological data analysis. Finally, the results of the research are presented in stage 7: theological evaluation.[8]

## The Limitations of the Pastoral Cycle

The pastoral cycle has been one of the foundational elements in teaching practical theology. Many find it helpful, but there are some problems with the method. The pastoral cycle tends to focus on occasions when there are problems in a pastoral context. This orientation toward tensions and conflict gives rise to significant drawbacks in the method. Most significantly, the cycle has a tendency to dislocate theological reflection from the ordinary ways in which the Christian church is continually engaged in connecting theology and practice. So theological reflection is placed outside the normal ways in which, by being part of the church, we are involved in the continual processes of theological reflection.

Educationalist Donald Schön describes the rich variety of ways in which professional practitioners engage in reflection. There are times when

7. Van der Ven, *Practical Theology*, 120.
8. Ibid., 119–56.

problem situations arise. Where this is the case the starting point of the pastoral cycle makes some sense. But there are a great many occasions where reflection is less intentional and structured. Practitioners, Schön says, reflect on their knowing-in-practice.[9] In other words, reflection is not so much a method to follow as part of the way that practitioners operate professionally. Sometimes, in the relative tranquility of a postmortem, they will think back on a project they have undertaken or a situation they have lived through and will explore the understandings they have brought to their handling of the case. They may do this in a mood of idle speculation or in a deliberate effort to prepare themselves for future cases.

Most frequently, reflection takes place in the midst of action. This reflection-in-action is conditioned by the constraints of the situation. It can be very rapid, or it might happen in minutes or even hours. For Schön, reflection is a complex process that is itself located within and in close relation to practice.[10] Schön's thinking seems to suggest that the pastoral cycle is a little programmatic, and his work indicates the extent to which reflection could perhaps be a much more dynamic and situated form of thinking.

There are criticisms of the pastoral cycle based on its origins. The cycle, as we have seen, has its roots in the social theory of Karl Marx. Cardijn and Freire were both influenced by Marxist thinking. Consequently, they see the process of education as one that enables those who are trapped in the social and economic relations of industrial society to become "aware" of their situation. And therefore through gaining knowledge they can become liberated. This approach to education rests on the Marxist notion that workers are largely ignorant or kept in the dark about the way the economic system controls workers. This assumption leads to an approach to education that is designed around the belief that there is always something under the surface and hidden to discover. The problem is that if you do not share this basic assumption and if you are not a Marxist, then the approach can seem rather alien at times.

There are also strong theological criticisms of the pastoral cycle. Two of the leading American practical theologians, Kathleen Cahalan and James Nieman, are deeply critical of the see-judge-act model and other

9. Schön, *Reflective Practitioner*, 61.
10. Ibid.

versions of the pastoral cycle and are uncomfortable with any model for practical theology that makes theology into one stage in a process. Practical theology, they argue, is theological throughout. This means that every stage in the method, if we think in terms of stages, must be grounded in the Christian faith. The pastoral cycle in its various versions implies that there are moments of analysis and understanding that are theologically neutral. This seems to imply that practitioners involved in ministry can in some way turn off their theological perspectives to analyze a situation. Not only does this seem unrealistic; it doesn't make sense. After all, the reason ministers do practical theology is that they are committed to the church. This does not go away for some stages and return for others; in fact, it shapes every aspect of reflection.

At the same time, the different versions of the pastoral cycle tend to situate theology as a normative moment, a place where theological judgments are made. The irony here, say Nieman and Cahalan, is that this in effect makes theology into simply the application of abstract principles, and it downplays the important ways theology is embedded in communities and practices.[11]

Despite these criticisms, the pastoral cycle can be very helpful. One of its significant values is that, in the context of formal education, it offers a structured way that habits of reflection can be encouraged and taught. Osmer's questions—What is going on? Why is this going on? What ought to be going on? How might we respond?—show how the various stages or "tasks" can be related in quite straightforward ways to the practice of ministry. Some of the theological problems with the cycle can be overcome by seeing it as a method that practitioners can take up and use as part of their ongoing theological reflection. So the starting point is not the method but the identity of the individual practitioner who is part of a community with its ongoing conversation about theology and practice.

## Theological Reflection That Doesn't Follow the Pastoral Cycle

Theological reflection does not have to follow the stages of the pastoral cycle. In fact, there are a great many studies in practical theology that make use of different methods, and all of them find a way to connect theology

11. Cahalan and Nieman, "Mapping the Field of Practical Theology," 84–85.

and practice. In the second part of this chapter, examples of theological reflection that do not follow the pastoral cycle are explored. These studies are of course interesting for what they tell us about the practice of the church, but they are also a significant resource for any student who has to design an extended piece of written work in practical theology. These different approaches offer a diverse range of methodological options that can be used to structure a written piece of work, whether it is a short assignment or a longer dissertation or thesis.

### Theological Reflection by Complexifying Practice

Not all approaches to theological reflection make use of the pastoral cycle in its entirety. An example of this is found in the work of John Swinton and Harriet Mowat. Practical theology, say Swinton and Mowat, finds its starting point in experience. As a result, it tends not to produce unified theological systems. "It uses the language of themes and patterns, rather than systems and universal concepts, seeking to draw us into the divine mystery." At the heart of this theological method lies a process of "complexifying" our understanding of situations and contexts. To complexify is to take something that is familiar and that we assume we understand and, through levels of analysis, to reveal the extent to which it is complex and multivalent. Situations, they argue, are "complex, multi-faceted entities which need to be examined with care, rigour and discernment if they are to be effectively understood."[12] Empirical research and particularly qualitative methods of inquiry are a means to explore situations in a more sustained and structured manner, offering multilayered and richly textured accounts of experience.

Swinton and Mowat illustrate their approach to practical theology and qualitative research through a series of case studies. One of these explores the area of hospital chaplaincy in Scotland. The study took place in 2003–2004, and all of the chaplains employed within the health service in Scotland were participants. The research, under the title *What Do Chaplains Do?*, set out to explore the "shifts in perspective and self-identification" being experienced by chaplains in Scotland. The data was collected first through telephone interviews with the chaplains. Then there were a series of case studies involving observation and informal interviews. These were

12. Swinton and Mowat, *Practical Theology and Qualitative Research*, 13.

then followed up by further telephone interviews. The research highlighted the extent to which hospital chaplains defined their role in relation to parish ministry. Often this comparison was framed in terms of a negative. So while parish ministers, for instance, were seen as being at the heart of the congregation, the church chaplains saw themselves, by contrast, as rather marginal in the health service.

At the same time, the research began to see ways in which chaplains developed a distinct sense of self. Central to this was the redefinition of their work in terms of spiritual care. Clergy working in parishes were seen primarily as ministers of the gospel who administered the Word and the sacraments to the congregation. Chaplains, however, were working in the less obviously Christian frameworks of the hospital, and so they had started to see themselves as spiritual caregivers. Some chaplains had started to position themselves as those who were "agenda free" in terms of religion, responding instead to a range of spiritualities. This raised the question for Swinton and Mowat about the coherence of chaplaincy in the hospital setting. If the chaplains are religiously neutral, then is there any specific need for them to be ordained ministers at all?[13]

This study of chaplaincy "complexifies" a practice, adding a depth of understanding and knowledge. The process of revealing in more depth what is taking place is shaped by theological concerns and perception, but it does not follow the typical stages of the pastoral cycle.

### Theological Reflection as a Form of Testing

One form of theological reflection starts with theological assertions and sets out to test how they work in practice. Here the starting point is different from both the traditional version of the pastoral cycle and the approach of Swinton and Mowat. Instead of a series of stages that start from experience, this approach sets out to interact with Christian ethics and systematic theology by asking critical questions about how theological ideas work out in communities and in practices.

Testing theological assertions lies at the heart of Christian Scharen's *Public Worship and Public Work*. Scharen's research has its roots in a growing consensus among liturgists and Christian ethicists that "Christian worship shapes people and communities committed to the broader public

---

13. Ibid., 180–87.

good, to acts of justice and peace in the world." The work of Stanley Hauerwas in particular has been deeply influential in the move toward these kinds of ideas in theology and Christian ethics. Worship, according to Hauerwas, is a social ethic, a public commitment par excellence. At the heart of this assertion lies a conviction that Aristotelian understandings of virtue or character ethics are enacted or made effective through engagement in Christian worship. So worship, it is argued, forms people for Christian living in the world.[14]

Scharen sets out to examine these theological assertions not by countering them with a contrasting conceptualization of worship and ethics but by embarking on an empirical study of actual worshiping congregations. Hauerwas and others, he admits, drew him to the idealistic framing of worship, but he wanted to know how these ideas worked out in actual congregations. So he designed his study to "test claims about the relation of worship and social-ethical commitment grounded in careful case studies of congregational life, worship and work."[15]

The research centered around three congregations in downtown Atlanta: the Catholic Shrine of the Immaculate Conception, Big Bethel African Methodist Episcopal, and Central Presbyterian. Scharen used a comparative extended case study approach to empirical methodology. The case study approach allows for the testing of theoretical issues, and it uses a range of ways to gather data. Scharen started by developing an understanding of the religious history of Atlanta through reading studies and histories. This was followed by four to five months of participant observation in each of the churches. This at first started with attending worship and talking informally with people in the congregation. Then, when he had gotten a sense for the church, Scharen would start to attend other kinds of meetings. Alongside the participant observation, there were a number of formal interviews conducted at each church. At each church, to supplement the interviews, a range of other materials was collected, such as worship programs, devotional guides, meeting handouts, membership directories, and educational material.

From the case studies, Scharen concludes that the prevailing understanding of the relationship between liturgy and social ethics is overly

14. Scharen, *Public Worship and Public Work*, 10.
15. Ibid.

"linear." By this he means that the effect of worship on character has often been portrayed in idealistic terms. When these issues are examined in actual communities, the rather simplistic linear understanding of how liturgy shapes behavior doesn't adequately explain what's happening. Most significantly, Scharen argues that the linear model has overlooked the crucial role of community life in the way that worship and social engagement operate at a local level. Scharen calls this the "profound structuring effect of a congregation's communal identity in relation to the church's public worship and work."[16] Communal life is actually sustained and developed not simply through the liturgy but through a range of different and complex sources. At the same time, the perception of what is "public" in the context of the local church is far from straightforward. Churches seem to have blurred edges, and so what is public is multiple and variegated.[17]

Worship itself, Scharen concludes, is for most people not so much formation as it is "con-formation, a reinforcement and reminder of what is important in life as they envision it in that place."[18] Liturgy therefore does not dramatically form or transform the individual Christian as a "moral agent." This does not mean that involvement in Christian communities has no effect on ethics but rather that its effect is mediated in multiple ways through the interaction of the complexity of communal life.

### Theological Reflection as a Way of Generating Theoretical Frameworks

James Fowler's book *Stages of Faith* has become one of the modern classics in practical theology. Fowler shifts the focus of theological discussion from doctrines and ecclesial formulations to the experience of individual believers. He constructs the category of faith as something that is not necessarily dependent on religion or belief. "Faith," says Fowler, "is a human universal. We are endowed at birth with nascent capacities for faith."[19] Fowler offers a theoretical framework for how faith grows and develops. He describes faith development as passing through a series of stages, beginning in early childhood (infancy is characterized by undifferentiated faith).

16. Ibid., 15.
17. Ibid., 15–16.
18. Ibid., 221.
19. Fowler, *Stages of Faith*, xiii.

Stage 1. Intuitive-projective faith (early childhood)

Stage 2. Mythic-literal faith (school years)

Stage 3. Synthetic-conventional faith (young adulthood)

Stage 4. Individuative-reflective faith (adulthood)

Stage 5. Conjunctive faith (mid-life and beyond)

Stage 6. Universalizing faith[20]

Fowler's theory of faith development as a series of stages grew initially from his own experience in clinical practice and from a critical engagement with psychological and education developmental theories. This enabled him to construct his notion of faith as a series of stages and transitions. As this work was being refined, the theoretical framework was tested through an extensive program of interview-based empirical research. The interviews involved a detailed conversation between the researcher and the participant.

The idea of faith development was not introduced as the purpose of the study; rather, participants were asked to share something of their attitudes and values as well as their life experiences. The research was based on 359 of these interviews conducted by different researchers over a nine-year period. The interviews yielded both qualitative and quantitative data. Qualitatively, the interviews provided descriptions of the stages and the transitions between stages. The interviews were also used to give a picture of the sample through quantitative analysis, which allowed the researchers to test for the relationship between different stages of faith.[21]

Fowler's research grew from clinical practice, but it enabled him to develop a way of viewing faith that has had a significant impact in practical theology. Again, Fowler does not use the pastoral cycle; rather, he investigates experience through empirical research to generate new theological insights that come from reflection on experience. In the pastoral cycle, theology is something that comes from beyond experience as a normative move based in the Scriptures in the tradition. In Fowler's work, a new theological construct arises from the investigation of practice and experience.

20. Ibid., 113.
21. Ibid., 311–23.

### Theological Reflection through the Worship of a Community

Mary McGann's *A Precious Fountain* explores the life and worship of Our Lady of Lourdes, an African American Catholic community in San Francisco. McGann calls her method "liturgical ethnography." "As such, it probes the rich particularity of one worshiping community whose roots and practice are at once Black and Catholic, using music as a primary lens through which to explore the community's liturgy and embodied theology."[22] The study is seen as part of a radical shift within Catholicism toward the embracing of difference and the enculturation of the gospel around the world. It is based on the belief that there is a hidden Spirit-given genius that lies within worshiping communities and that the church needs in particular to learn from the life and worship of multiethnic congregations.[23]

The research was conducted over five years (1993–97) and is based on McGann's involvement in the worshiping life of the congregation. She draws on actual worship events—what she calls "the complex interplay of musical sound, movements, gestures, speech, objects, dress, time, space, light, and color." Added to this data drawn from participant observation are a number of interviews with musicians, worshipers, and clergy. In addition to these interviews, a range of informal conversations took place around the worship that McGann draws on. Her purpose, she says, "is to offer a 'picture of the landscape of meanings' experienced by the community as they emerge within the 'logic of lived musical and liturgical experience, a logic that is not primarily linear but interactive, dynamic, and holistic.'"[24]

Liturgical ethnography, says McGann, is a spiritual discipline. It demands a prayerful attention to the other. Attending to music in worship involves the ability to be with a congregation without making judgments, "until you flow with the rhythm, the pace of its action; until your interior metronome is beating with theirs."[25] Communities carry in their worship a lived logic wisdom, and writing ethnography is a contemplative process of receiving this embodied wisdom.

Central to the research was the adoption of what McGann calls "a Black hermeneutic." To understand the worship of this community, it is

22. McGann, *Precious Fountain*, xv.
23. Ibid., xvi.
24. McGann, *Exploring Music*, 43, quoted in ibid., xix.
25. McGann, *Precious Fountain*, xix.

necessary to adopt particular interpretive frameworks. These are carried in part within the worship of Our Lady of Lourdes, but they are also seen in the perspectives of black theologians and scholars of black music. This hermeneutic is based on the perspective that African music and the cultural practices and rituals that surround it survived the dislocation of slavery, and this African cultural element has continued to shape black music and worship.

Black Americans, she argues, were converted through a "twisted" version of Christianity, but through the reexpression of faith influenced by African musical forms they were able to "retwist" the faith into a version of Christianity that was characterized by liberation, transcendence, creativity, and wholeness. "This Black hermeneutic posits that African American music is the most comprehensive repository of Black theology in the United States; that within this tradition, music, narrative, and ritual are traditional forms of systematic theology, and that singing, dancing and drumming in worship are not simply stylistic elements, incidental to a community's practice, but profoundly theological acts in and of themselves."[26]

Music lies at the heart of the study precisely because for African Americans it carries within it deep intuitions about their sense of self and about the wider world. Music, she explains, "establishes a set of relationships—person to person, individual to society, humanity to the natural and supernatural world—and it is in those relationships that the meaning of the act lies." For black Americans, music plays a crucial role in their sense of identity and their cultural memory. It carries theology and spirituality through participatory forms of musical expression. It is the fountain from which comes the desire to hold together in a holistic sensibility what it is to be black and American. From this source spring the distinctive rituals of Christian worship, social relations, and living faith that characterize the community.[27]

At the start of her study, McGann makes it clear that she is a nonblack American woman. Her understanding of black theology and worship has come to her through study in later life and through her own participation in African American styles of worship. Her attempt to interpret

26. Ibid., xx.
27. Ibid., xxi.

the community, she makes clear, is a collaborative venture. Her insights and various kinds of analysis have developed in dialogue with her fellow worshipers. When she wrote up her research, she formed a group of four people, including worship leaders, clergy, and laypeople from the church, who helped her edit her work.

### Theological Reflection on the Self through Narration

Practical theologian Heather Walton has been developing an approach to empirical research that draws on auto-ethnography and narrative. She uses literary and autobiographical accounts of her own personal history to explore an embodied and lived theology. Her highly creative approach to empirical research is illustrated in her discussion of preaching and vocation. Walton's writing consists of recollections of preaching. She recounts these as short narratives, including one in which she tells of her friendship with someone she met while he was training for ministry. He had been a dog handler in the Royal Air Force at the time she had been a protestor. So they had been on different sides of the fence. She was asked to preach at his ordination. On that day, she says,

> The swords had become ploughshares and teams were already at work ploughing up the gardens ready for the great harvest. Inside the church, between the aisles, the wolf pack lay dozing. The leader cradled a sleeping lamb between his giant paws while the rest of the softly bleating flock were penned behind the altar rails. The tree of life was pushing up tough, thick roots right through the floorboards and the new leaves on the branches were for the healing of the nations, and I felt the Spirit descending like a dove. She placed an olive branch in my hands and there was such glory in the radiance of her wings. "See how today all these words have been fulfilled in your sight," I said. And all the people said "Amen."[28]

Walton also movingly recounts how she found herself speaking to a full church. The pews were all occupied; it was standing room only. The people had gathered for the funeral of a baby, and at the front of the church was a small white coffin. The mother was a friend, and Walton had been asked to give the address. The words, she says, were not her own; they had been given to her. She had offered her voice to her friend.

28. Walton, "Calls to Preach," 65.

Through the service Walton says that she had not allowed herself to
share in the grief of those who were present. She had a job to do, "a
serious job to do that required me not to feel but to speak." The words
she was asked to speak joined the mourners' pain to the suffering of
mothers in Palestine, in the Gulf States, and in Bosnia. The words placed
"our sweet child in the company of other holy innocents." The whole of
creation was groaning with these words, and "I spoke them clearly and
calmly and I did not falter until I had almost reached the end." Trying to
make sense of this experience, Walton was reminded of a small ceramic
statue she had once found in a museum. The figure was labeled *The
Prophet*. The prophet was wearing a loosely stitched costume. Walton
says, "My stomach lurched when I read the inscription, 'The prophet is
clothed in the skins of the dead.' The reason I felt this wrenching in my
guts was because I knew what I had read was true."[29] For the preacher,
sometimes the words she speaks are not her own. Then she is clothed in
the skin of those who are silent. "I have not travelled there often. Just
a few times."[30]

The purpose behind these explorations into the experience of preaching lies in Walton's desire to make sense of her calling, which she calls
a "retrospective theology." It is not so much made up of systematic or
even ordered thought but is "passionately formed out of vivid moments
in which I experienced calls to preach." The use of narrative in this form
of recollection allows Walton to pay attention to the various details that
surround an experience. It leads to a genre of expression that is hospitable
to "deeply metaphorical language," and it is in these linguistic forms that
Walton feels she is able to address the sacredness of her experience.[31]

Through her writing Walton says she has created "fictions of faith."
These are attempts to recontextualize preaching in material, ecclesial,
communal, and political contexts. They present an image of the preacher
"as having been given voice through her body." This leads to a celebratory incarnational theology. The body of the preacher is not defined by
lineage or by blood. Hers is "a spiritual body in which the mystery of God
is encountered dwelling among us in glory."[32]

29. Ibid., 66.
30. Ibid., 67.
31. Ibid., 64.
32. Ibid., 73.

### Theological Reflection through Pastoral Practice

In *Ethnography as a Pastoral Practice*, Mary Clark Moschella argues for empirical research as a "tool" in theological reflection in the context of ministerial practice. Ethnography, she argues, can help leaders hear the wisdom of the people; it can open up conversations that can transform how things work in a community. Ethnography is a means to immerse oneself in the life of people to learn something about them and from them. As a pastoral practice, ethnography involves listening and care. Its foundation lies in the significance of the stories that people tell. "We shape our lives and give meaning and coherence to them through telling personal stories. Likewise, we are shaped by the familial, cultural, and religious stories that we hear—from parents, schools, media, and houses of worship—all around us."[33]

Central to Moschella's vision for ethnography is that it should be used as a part of pastoral practice. Empirical research, she argues, positions the leader as a "learner" in the community. Paying attention to the sights, smells, and tastes of communal life will lead the pastor into a much richer and more complex understanding of the cultural narratives of the community in which he or she serves. This kind of attention will enable the pastor to "read" the culture of the congregation with much more sensitivity. "In these ways, the practice of ethnographic research can become a form of holistic pastoral listening that attends to the range of meanings, experiences, desires, and theologies that congregations express not only through their words but also through their lives."[34]

Moschella positions ethnography as itself part of a pastoral and caring ministry. In a therapeutic context, stories become the means to healing and wholeness. Moschella sees ethnographic research as a means by which individuals and communities, through storytelling, can be engaged in a coauthoring process—through sharing in the development of a corporate story. This practice can in turn lead toward the reevaluation or reenvisioning of communal self-description. "Listening to complex local stories can help a congregation get unstuck from the tyranny of tradition and the ubiquitous reasoning of 'We've never done it that way before!'"[35]

33. Moschella, *Ethnography as a Pastoral Practice*, 5.
34. Ibid., 10.
35. Ibid., 6.

The pastor offers care through research by being the listener. "I stress the practice of listening because I believe that deep down, listening is a liberating practice, a practice that validates and honors another person's experience, insight and soul." Ethnography therefore becomes a way to help groups through listening and calling forth stories. Listening is not simply passive. There are forms of listening that are "reflective." This initiates a dialogical process of hearing stories and reflecting these back so that they may in turn be revised and corrected. In the context of caring relationship, this process can be the means toward transformation and healing.[36]

## Patterns for Theological Reflection

Theological reflection is a mainstay in courses in practical theology. In many instances, training in practical theology focuses on teaching a version of the pastoral cycle. Yet the pastoral cycle, as we have seen, is not the only way to reflect theologically on practice. The examples that have been discussed show that practical theology actually takes a number of different forms. It is not necessary, for instance, to start with experience. Christian Scharen's work starts with Christian ethics and then explores how particular theological ideas work out in practice. None of the examples structure their work by passing through "stages" of the pastoral cycle. Instead, there are a variety of ways of investigating practice and different ways of engaging with theological themes.

A number of the examples make use of empirical methods such as ethnography, observation, and interviews to uncover the richness in practice. Swinton and Mowat, for instance, use empirical research to enable them to see into the complex dynamics and ways of operating for chaplains working in a hospital setting. Their study analyzes experience through data gathered by researchers and then uses this data to develop a nuanced account of what chaplains do. James Fowler's *Stages of Faith* is similar in that it explores the phenomena of faith through interviews and develops a more complex account than had previously been the case. Both of these studies leave hanging the question of theological normativity. It is one thing to say what chaplains do but another to ask, what should they do? It is interesting to note, however, that even though Fowler's *Stages of*

36. Ibid., 13.

*Faith* does not explore what faith should be, since it was written it has itself been used quite frequently as a normative account of faith.

Involvement in the life of the church can itself become a place for formal and structured kinds of theological reflection. Mary Moschella writes about the various ways in which ministers in their daily pastoral situations can engage in practice-based research. This kind of empirically oriented attention to pastoral encounters becomes an enriching and renewing activity in ministry. Mary McGann turns her participation in a congregation into a lengthy and detailed study. The community's worship becomes the place for theological reflection. She uses interviews and analysis of songs, music, and practices, but the heart of the research comes from her own participation as a worshiper in a particular community. From this she is able to give a detailed account of how theological themes are performed and enacted in the life of the church. These examples show the diversity of possibilities, but in the end the real challenge in theological reflection is that we are each expected to be able to do it.

## Theological Reflection: Some Guidelines

Most people first encounter theological reflection as an expectation. It could be during a training course, or when we join a team of practitioners, or as part of a parish study day with theological reflection on the agenda. In these circumstances, when there appears to be an expectation that we should stop normal life and reflect theologically, it is worth having some guidelines to orient ourselves.

1. *Some ambiguity is to be expected.* The first thing to remember is that theological reflection is not straightforward, and so it is highly likely that the leaders of the session have at best a hazy idea of what they mean by theological reflection. If they seem to be clear about the process and they present it as a series of predetermined stages or steps, then they probably haven't thought about what they are doing very deeply. So don't be intimidated or, indeed, fooled.

2. *Theological reflection is a natural and normal part of our lives.* The next thing to do is to remind yourself that while you may not be an expert in all the different methods of theological reflection, just by being part of the church you have absorbed a number of sophisticated

ways of thinking about practice and theology. So when asked to reflect theologically, it is worthwhile to spend a few moments thinking through the occasions during the last few weeks when you have thought about God and life. This may have been while singing a hymn, in the car driving home from work, when you were praying, or when you were reading the paper. Don't think just about what you thought but also about the way you were thinking. This will suggest methods of theological reflection that work best for you. It does not mean that you might not find other ways to reflect, but it gives you an orientation so you do not feel that you are suddenly in alien territory. Remind yourself that you know how to do this, because you do it naturally and with some skill.

3. *Theological reflection is grounded in everyday life and ministry.* Most of the issues people have with theological reflection come from encountering it in the classroom or at training events. Because theological reflection is most often taught in a classroom setting, it can seem to be slightly disconnected from the everyday events of church life and ministerial practice. This is the opposite of the intention, but it is frankly quite hard to overcome the dynamics of the classroom. Donald Schön's exploration of the various ways that practitioners think about practice is a reminder that reflection should never be seen as an end in itself. Reflection should arise from, and have a location in, what is happening. In other words, the key to developing theological reflection is found not in following a method but in practice itself. This means that it is almost impossible to teach theological reflection in a group that is not already, and with some immediacy, engaged in some form of ministry. Theological reflection cannot realistically be summoned out of the air.

4. *Methods should be derived from a specific problematic.* The variety of different studies that we have explored in this chapter (and there are of course many more to discover) show how theological reflection can work in very different ways. There is no single way to reflect theologically. So the question arises, how should we go about reflecting? The answer lies not in following a methodology but in being clear about what prompts us to reflect. The issue dictates the method. Issues are those things that nag at us from time to time. They

are things that don't add up, places where the shoe seems to rub just a little, or strategies that don't work. Issues need to be real and not invented for the sake of, say, fulfilling academic requirements. They need to have a certain amount of urgency about them. Theological reflection for its own sake will always feel fake and a little pointless.

5. *Use the method that seems to work best.* Having gained some clarity about the issue, it may be hard to come up with a method for reflection. One way to proceed is to run through different examples of theological reflection to look for a problem or an issue that is similar to the one you are wrestling with. With a similar issue, it might be possible to simply follow the approach that seems to work in the example. Having said this, it is always a good thing to try to develop or adapt ways of working so they fit your project more closely.

6. *Put yourself into the study.* Whatever the specific issue and whatever your chosen method, it is important to spend some time thinking about yourself. Think through how you have been shaped and formed as part of the Christian church. Try to identify how specific experiences of theological perspectives that you carry with you might help to shape or indeed pull out of shape your attempt at theological reflection. If this is a piece of writing, then putting yourself into the study in specific ways may not simply be desirable—it might be essential. After all, this study must matter to you or be of importance to you for some reason. Naming this is a fundamental part of theological reflection.

7. *Step back periodically and assess your work.* Even the most experienced researchers will, from time to time, get lost in their research. The detail can be overwhelming, or a particular line of thinking can take over. Before you know it, you find that you have gone off course or even gotten lost. To address this issue, it is worth stepping back occasionally and asking if what you are doing is still on track. Two kinds of problems in theological reflection appear with some regularity. Researchers either become so interested in practice that they fail to find a way to connect to theology, or they become so absorbed in theological work that they forget to make specific connections to practice. In other words, the central problematic of practical theology—namely, how to relate practice and theology—comes

apart. Given the amount of agonizing and debate over this issue, it really shouldn't come as a surprise that students and practitioners might struggle occasionally. In fact, it should be expected that this problem would almost certainly appear at some point.

8. *Choose your method wisely and discuss the reasons for your choice.* Writing theological reflection entails a number of decisions. Much of the conversation so far has been around method in practical theology. One thing to conclude from this is that making a decision about method is crucial. Method should follow the research issues and specific research questions, but when making this decision it is nearly always a good idea to spend time thinking of alternatives. If you have to write a methodology section in your paper, for instance, talking through methods that won't work or are flawed in some way is almost as important as setting out your chosen approach. Discussion of methods is one way to show that you understand some of the central questions in practical theology and also that you have a grasp of the literature.

9. *Structure your reflection appropriately.* The crucial difference between discussing and writing theological reflection is that writing is necessarily linear. When we are writing, we are forced to make decisions about the order in which we present material. The pastoral cycle is helpful because it sets out a clear progression for theological reflection, but there are other ways of structuring a piece of writing. Different structures will enable a written piece of work to do different things. So, for instance, if it starts with a theological discussion, this can be tested by examining practice, whereas a more normative function for theology would generally mean that it is situated after the presentation of practice. Method and structure enable different kinds of theological reflection.

10. *Practical theology exists to serve the church.* Finally, with all the concern about methods and approaches to writing, it is very easy to lose sight of the reason we are doing theological reflection. Practical theology, even in an academic context, exists to serve the church. It is part of the church's conversation about its life and the life of God. It is important, then, not to lose sight of this overarching calling to the church and to those of us doing theology on behalf of the Christian community.

# 7

# Practical Theology and Theological Disciplines

There is a temptation, especially when you are starting out, to regard practical theology as consisting of those who label themselves practical theologians and the books they write. This, however, is a mistake. As has already been mentioned in chapter 5, the origins of practical theology lie in the education of clergy. Traditionally, there have been five related fields of inquiry that made up clerical education: the study of preaching (homiletics), the study of worship (liturgics), the study of church order, the study of pastoral care, and the study of Christian education. While in some parts of the world this understanding of what constitutes practical theology remains the dominant model, it is also the case that these areas of study have become academic fields of study in their own right. So, for instance, the study of worship has developed its own conferences and journals. The same is true for homiletics and Christian education. These developments have brought about a wealth of research and thinking that does not actually label itself as practical theology. Taking my working definition of practical theology—namely, study that takes seriously both practice and theology—it is clear that the net is much wider than those who explicitly call themselves practical theologians.

The realization that practical theology is much larger than those scholars who identify themselves as practical theologians is an important insight. You might actually have read quite a lot of books and shared ideas and thinking that can be seen as practical theology without realizing it. A good example is the writing that has been generated within the gospel and culture movement and around the mission of the church. The next chapter explores some of this material in more detail, but my point here is this: to the extent that a book about, for instance, the missional church or leadership and discipleship in contemporary culture deals with both practice and theology, it is (in my estimation) practical theology, even if the authors do not regard themselves as part of the discipline. Realizing that practical theology is much more common and is a shared perspective across different fields of study extends beyond the traditional five areas of preaching, worship, church organization, pastoral care, and Christian education. In recent years there has been a move toward practice that is evident across a range of disciplines within the study of religion and theology. These developments are significant for practical theology because they generate significant common ground among areas of work that have often been seen as quite different and distinct.

In an academic context, practical theology is generally studied alongside a number of interrelated theological disciplines. These include the core theological disciplines of biblical studies, doctrine, Christian ethics, and church history, as well as various kinds of social scientific study of religion (e.g., religious studies, the sociology of religion, and anthropology). While there are differences of approach and emphasis, each of these areas of study is complementary and helpful to practical theology because the life, belief, and practice of the church are central to the interests and concerns of each one of these areas. Practical theology should never be undertaken in a disciplinary vacuum. There must always be moments in which biblical, doctrinal, historical, or social scientific insights and approaches are not only helpful but essential.

In chapter 5 we saw how both Clement Rogers and Seward Hiltner argued that the academic disciplines traditionally associated with theology need to be oriented toward a pastoral perspective if they are to be used by ministers as part of practical theology. The idea that the disciplines need to be adapted or reoriented toward practice reflects something of a tension that is often felt within practical theology toward the more traditional disciplines. This tension comes from a widely held perception that theology has often been a conversation that has ignored the practice of the church. Practical theology has therefore tended to present itself as something of a corrective to the more abstract or obtuse forms of theological thinking.

Practical theology has kept blue water between itself and other theological disciplines by arguing that it starts from experience and is rooted in the embodied practice of the church. There are two problems with this. The first is that there are significant approaches to practical theology that are more applied in method—that is, they start with the Bible or doctrine and then move toward practice. The other problem is that across the range of disciplines within theology and religious studies, there has been a remarkable shift toward practice.

In this chapter I look at examples from biblical studies, doctrinal theology, church history, and religious studies and the social sciences. It is impossible to do justice to such a wide range of disciplines in this short chapter, and so my intention is to offer brief snapshots from particular authors and then show how these writers are moving into areas that are very close to the interests, concerns, and methods of practical theology. In doing this, I am not arguing that a biblical scholar or a church historian is a practical theologian; rather, I want to illustrate that there is now a shared interest in practice, culture, and communities and that this makes it much easier for practical theology to draw directly on the more established theological disciplines. Particularly for students starting out in practical theology, this should enable them to see connections between their different areas of study.

## Biblical Studies

Biblical studies has traditionally focused on biblical texts. It has involved the study of biblical and other ancient languages as well as the literary and theological analysis of individual books and letters in the Bible. In practical theology, the Bible is a key reference point, providing a critical, constructive, and normative voice from the Christian tradition to the contemporary situation. The critical and analytical tools developed in biblical studies provide a vital resource for this enterprise, but recent developments in biblical studies have meant that there is a significant crossover of interests between the discipline and practical theology.

The first of these developments is the rise of what has been called the sociology of the New Testament. The move toward sociology in New Testament studies is in part a reaction to the sense that the "history of ideas and words" approach that once characterized much of the work in the field seemed to deny or at least overlook the significance of communities and cultural contexts that formed such an important part of the texts. One of the most significant works in this area is Wayne Meeks's *The First Urban Christians: The Social World of the Apostle Paul*. While Meeks does not at all intend to make direct connections to the practice of the present-day church, he develops a picture of the social context of the New Testament in such a way that parallels could more easily be drawn between the ecclesiology and missiological life of the early church and the present-day church. This move, then, has served to make biblical studies more accessible to missional and practical theologians who are concerned with the social shape of the church by allowing the sociology of the New Testament to feed into conversations around the gospel and contemporary culture as well as the debates around new missional forms of church.

A second development in biblical studies that is of central importance for practical theology is the movement toward what has been called the theological interpretation of Scripture. This approach to reading the Bible is an attempt to address the tendency in biblical studies to seemingly lock the text in self-contained conversation among scholars around the historically specific meaning of the text. Theological approaches to biblical interpretation foreground the idea that the primary purpose of Scripture is to inform and generate theological perspectives for the Christian community in the present. The process of biblical interpretation is therefore seen as being a movement guided by the Holy Spirit where theologians seek understanding and truth.

This approach can be seen in the work of Daniel J. Treier and Stephen Fowl.[1] Fowl argues that Scripture should be read through a theological understanding of its nature. "Christians are committed to the notion that Scripture is the word of God. In, through, or in spite of its clearly human, historical characteristics, Christians confess that Scripture repeats, conveys, or reflects the words of the living God. At the very least, this makes Scripture the

---

1. See Treier, *Introducing Theological Interpretation of Scripture*; Fowl, *Theological Interpretation*.

standard against which Christian faith and practice need to measure up."[2] This move toward the present-day role of Scripture in the church is deeply significant for practical theology because it means that biblical scholars and practical theologians are sharing similar concerns and interests. This, then, is a further example of the convergence in theological studies around practice.

A third important development in biblical studies has been a growing interest in the reception of Scripture. This has taken two main forms. There has been a concerted interest in the historic reception of Scripture, and in the last few years a number of important empirical studies have centered on how the contemporary church interprets Scripture. In *Congregational Hermeneutics: How Do We Read?*, Andrew Rogers explores the contrasting ways that Christians speak about the Bible. Through a series of qualitative congregational studies, Rogers shows how the practice of biblical interpretation in small groups, for instance, can often diverge from or even contradict the doctrinal position that is advocated by the church. Rogers comes from a practical theology background, but his work crosses the boundaries between biblical studies and practical theology and demonstrates again the convergence of the fields.

## Doctrinal Theology

In recent years, there has also been a marked turn in doctrinal theology toward practice and the church as the key locus of theological discussion. Debates around the doctrine of the Trinity, for instance, have incorporated notions of relationship and community as central to their themes.[3] Influential theologians such as Stanley Hauerwas have emphasized the importance of the Christian community and its ongoing practice of worship for both doctrine and ethics. These kinds of developments have been taken up in the conversation that has arisen around the contribution that empirical work might bring to ecclesiology.

Roman Catholic systematic theologian Nicholas Healy has been a key voice in this conversation. In 2000 Healy called for what he referred to as a practical-prophetic ecclesiology. Central to the kind of ecclesiology he

2. Fowl, *Theological Interpretation*, 2.
3. See, e.g., Volf, *After Our Likeness*; Zizioulas, *Being as Communion*. In recent scholarship, there has been significant rethinking of this position. See Kilby, "Perichoresis and Projection"; Kilby, "Is an Apophatic Trinitarianism Possible?"; and Holmes, "Three versus One?"

envisions is a turn toward ethnography. Healy argues that ecclesiology should consider the "concrete response" of the church to its Lord by making use of notions of culture. He accepts that social scientific studies of the church have been undertaken for many years, but he argues that these did not ask specifically theological questions, or at least that they did not ask the kind of questions that were of pressing interest to theologians. Healy concludes that "the church needs to introduce its own, theological form of cultural analysis, which we can call ecclesiological ethnography."[4] This interest in ethnography has been echoed by a number of other theologians.[5]

Two volumes have emerged from the interest in ethnography among theologians: *Perspectives in Ecclesiology and Ethnography* and *Explorations in Ecclesiology and Ethnography*. These volumes focus on the methodological possibilities and limits of an ecclesiology that is both empirical and theological.[6] In them, writers from different theological positions explore the relationships between the kind of knowledge that is produced through qualitative empirical research and the ways of knowing and seeing that are appropriate within theology.[7] Within the ecclesiology and ethnography conversation, there is a convergence around empirical research as part of a developing doctrine of the church. The shared interest in this work crosses boundaries among anthropologists, systematic theologians, sociologists of religion, and practical theologians. The boundaries separating these disciplines appear more porous as a result of shared interests and shared methodological approaches.

These developments are significant for practical theology because they show how different academics are working in ways that are very similar. In other words, what is emerging is a shared conversation around theology and practice where different disciplines learn from each other and share insights. Within this context, practical theology is not set apart from the more traditional theological disciplines but is seen as having a contributing role.

4. Healy, *Church, World and the Christian Life*, 168–69.
5. See, e.g., Scharen, "Judicious Narratives"; Fulkerson, *Places of Redemption*.
6. For material from the ecclesiology and ethnography conversation, see the journal *Ecclesial Practices* (Leiden: Brill). See also Scharen and Vigen, *Ethnography as Christian Theology and Ethics*; Ward, *Perspectives on Ecclesiology and Ethnography*; and Scharen, *Explorations in Ecclesiology and Ethnography*. A number of publications seek to bring together empirical and theological perspectives on the church, including Hegstad, *Real Church*; and Ormerod, *Re-Visioning the Church*.
7. This debate has now led to monographs exploring these issues. E.g., Scharen, *Fieldwork in Theology*. See also Hegstad, *Real Church*.

## Church History

Starting with Eusebius in the fourth century, church history has played a central role in a theological understanding of the church. Bede's *Ecclesiastical History of the English People*, written in the eighth century, did not simply offer an account of events in the past; it offered a vision for national identity and the place of the church in the developing story of a nation. In more recent times, developments in historical study mean that it also is starting to share significant territory and interests with practical theology. Historical research has for some time been interested in the way religion has been lived and practiced. Two examples of this are the work of Eamon Duffy and the work of Jane Shaw.

In *The Stripping of the Altars*, Duffy recounts how, before the Reformation, in communities across England, Catholic images, art, and rituals were embedded in the lives of individuals and communities. During the Reformation, these material forms of religion were turned over in favor of a new Protestant theological sensibility. Duffy describes the impact of this change on congregations across England. He shows how individuals sought to preserve aspects of their previous religion and how they renegotiated their sense of self in the middle of this radical change.

Duffy's work is not explicitly practical theology, but it does share an interest in theology and practice. He clearly portrays how religion was experienced and lived by communities in England in the sixteenth century. So while Duffy works with the past, his methods and interest cross over in significant ways with how practical theologians study communities in the present. In fact, the close attention to material objects as part of the lives of believers is suggestive of ways that those of us interested in the present-day church might develop our work.

In her book *Octavia, Daughter of God: The Story of a Female Messiah and Her Followers*, historian Jane Shaw paints a vivid picture of the Panacea Society, a community started early in the twentieth century by Mabel Barltrop, who was believed by her followers to be a messiah. Shaw combines interviews of surviving members of the group with insights gleaned from a previously unexamined archive kept by the society in their communal house in Bedford, England. What emerges is an account of a community that, at its height, reached out through its healing ministry to more than one hundred and thirty thousand people all around the world but had dwindled to only two remaining members. Shaw speaks of the way she was drawn into the life of the group, fascinated by the gossip and dynamics of this community. Shaw calls her work a life, or a biography, of the community itself.

The work of Duffy and of Shaw is academic and historical in nature. As such, it does not make explicit connections between the contemporary church and the communities they describe, but a common thread running through their work is the sense that these historical accounts of lived religion are significant because in recovering the past we understand something of ourselves in the present.

Ian Bradley's book *Celtic Christianity: Making Myths and Chasing Dreams*, by way of contrast, deliberately sets out to discuss the significance of church history for the contemporary church. Bradley argues that what has been called Celtic Christianity has been continuously revised and revisited over the years. The "golden age" of Celtic Christianity is generally seen as being between the mid-fifth and the mid-seventh centuries. It is associated with the Irish and British saints Patrick, Brigit, Ninian, Columba, and Aidan, and the holy sites of Clonmacnoise, Derry, Iona, Llanwit Major, and Lindisfarne. This was the age that gave birth to intricate, illuminated manuscripts, stories of monks and missionaries, and a spirituality rooted in nature and wild places.[8] For many in the contemporary church, Celtic Christianity represents a refreshing spiritual alternative to what might be seen as more modern or possibly shallow forms of Christianity. The legacy of the Celtic world, by contrast, appears to offer deep roots in a theology and forms of spiritual practice that have a connection in the past.[9]

Bradley sets this search for Celtic roots in a historical perspective. He points out that the church over the centuries has been drawn back to rediscover Celtic Christianity. The first such rediscovery dates back to the Venerable Bede, who argued in *Life of Cuthbert* that the saint's life was a stark contrast to the corruption of the church in the ninth century. In the twelfth and thirteenth centuries, there was another revival in interest; Celtic Christianity was seen to connect to the popularity of the Arthurian legends and the quest for the Grail. In the Reformation, the Celtic church was regarded as an inspiration to an English church apart from Rome,

8. Bradley, *Celtic Christianity*, 1.
9. Ibid., ix.

and later in the nineteenth century the Romantic revival embraced the Celtic church.[10]

Bradley's point is that at various moments the interest in Celtic Christianity has emerged as an inspiration to Christians, and the present-day revival fits into this pattern of rediscovery. "A persistent vein of nostalgia has allowed those Christians who lived in the sixth and seventh centuries, about whose faith and work we know next to nothing first hand, to become paragons of a pure and primitive faith."[11] The point here is that there is an element of projection on the past and a re-creation of these Celtic figures in ways that mirror the particular interests and concerns of each new revival.

From the work of Duffy, Shaw, and Bradley, it is evident that historians are deeply concerned with the experience and practice of lived religion. These interests are of course focused in the past, but this does not mean that they are fundamentally different from the ways of thinking and researching that are common in practical theology. Practical theology focuses on the present day, but the methods and kinds of material that emerge from research and thinking are remarkably similar to those that are commonplace in the study of history. History, of course, has always to some extent been a conversation about the present, as issues of identity and social life are reworked by examining common roots and problems. This kind of political or social commentary, it should be noted, is also a point of convergence between church history and practical theology.

## Religious Studies and the Social Sciences

In the study of religion and in the social sciences there has been a renewed interest in the study of Christianity and the practice of the church. We have already discussed Meredith McGuire's treatment of lived religion. Set alongside this work is the development of the anthropology of Christianity, which has received considerable attention in recent years.[12] T. M. Luhrmann's writing is an excellent example of the interest in Christianity among contemporary anthropologists. In *When God Talks Back*, Luhrmann gives an account of an extended ethnographic study of Vineyard

10. Ibid., viii.
11. Ibid., ix.
12. See Fennell, *Anthropology of Christianity*.

churches in North America. Her central concern is to investigate how members of these churches learn to hear the voice of God in their everyday lives. From this starting point, what develops is an in-depth discussion of the practices and theological culture of prayer within the charismatic community. Robert Orsi is another important figure writing in the area of religious studies. Orsi has pioneered approaches to the study of religious communities that combine historical, ethnographic, and theological forms of analysis.[13]

What is clear in the work of scholars such as Luhrmann and Orsi is that the interests and concerns of those studying Christian communities in the social sciences have considerable crossover with the interests of practical theologians. This kind of crossover is also evident in the work of another scholar: Robert Beckford. Beckford is a theologian who makes use of cultural studies and musicology to explore the links between popular culture and theology. His work shows how different disciplines merge in the study of contemporary religion.

In *Jesus Is Dread*, Beckford discusses the music of Bob Marley and the significance of Rastafarianism. For Beckford, as a black Christian growing up in Britain, Marley's music was both controversial and inspirational. He acknowledges that this music was unacceptable to his parents and that Rastafarianism was forbidden by them. Nonetheless, like many other young black Christians, Beckford identified with this music. In Marley's songs he found clues to his own identity, history, and social situation.[14] He recognizes that this was a tension he lived with, and he admits that occasionally he preached against Marley and Rastafarianism. At this later stage in his life, he wants to explore the theological significance of Marley. "Today things are very different. Not only do I continue to appreciate reggae music, but I am acutely aware of its political and religious significance in Britain. In the light of this, I want to suggest that a critical appropriation of Rastafari has much to offer the Black Church in Britain today" (*JD*, 116).

Beckford suggests that reggae music may become an important theological resource for black Christians. In particular, he explores Marley as a liberation theologian by examining a selection of Marley's songs recorded between 1973 and 1983. His starting point is what he identifies as Marley's theological method, which he examines under three main headings.

13. See Orsi, *Madonna of 115th Street*.
14. Beckford, *Jesus Is Dread*, 115 (hereafter cited in text as *JD*).

First, Marley's songs move from a black experience of life toward a critique of white-dominated social systems such as education—or "head-decay-shun," as it appears in the song "Four Hundred Years" on the *Catch a Fire* album. Meaning is derived for Marley from experience. This is illustrated, says Beckford, in the *Natty Dread* album, where in the title track Marley speaks of "Natty Dreadlocks" walking through Jamaican streets. Beckford interprets this as representative of an inner journey within levels of consciousness toward a sense of black identity and historical belonging (*JD*, 118).

Second, Marley advocates a radical social change. Beckford views this as a concern to see the destruction of the alienating system represented in Marley's lyrics by the song "Babylon." At the same time, in "Redemption Song" Marley appears to advocate a more psychological transformation of the individual. Marley is also highly committed to the emancipation of the poor.

The third aspect of Marley's method, according to Beckford, relates to reggae music itself. "Reggae music emerges from the urban proletariat in Jamaica. It is the descendant of slave music, containing the survivals of slave rhythms and songs. Reggae music reveals that the medium in which theology is expressed is itself significant for communicating the meaning of God." Beckford relates the musical significance of reggae to the place of music in the black church. Here the presence of the Spirit is experienced in song. Songs therefore can be seen as anointed in the black Pentecostal tradition (*JD*, 121).

These three themes in Marley's work relate to biblical theology. The notion of experience is read by Beckford as an inner revelation, which then seeks confirmation in the Bible (*JD*, 122). Thus when Marley says that "Jah seh"—in which "Jah," meaning "God," is a shortened form of the word "Jahweh"—there is an assertion of revelation. The Bible is used to locate this insight. Rastafarianism sees this method in the links made between the assertion of the divinity of the emperor of Ethiopia and the biblical royal line of David. Beckford is clear that the biblical basis for Rastafarian claims concerning Selassie are less than convincing. As an orthodox Christian he is therefore critical of the theological construction within Rastafarianism. He is more approving of similar links that are built between biblical stories of exodus and the Rastafarian yearning for a return to Africa. Marley's song "Exodus" speaks of a dissatisfaction with life as it is lived and calls for a departure from "Babylon." This is the exodus: a movement of God's people (*JD*, 123).

Beckford sees these themes as an illustration of the theological creativity of Marley. While he is not a traditional theologian, says Beckford, Marley is a liberation theologian, or at least he is a Rastafarian theologian whose work represents a resource for black Christians. Beckford argues that Marley's music is a reminder to black Christians that theology is linked to issues of power and ideology. In Marley's view, to refuse to stand up for the rights of the poor and the dispossessed is to be less than human. At the same time, Beckford is critical of Marley's relations with women, and he is mindful of the feminist critique of the rock star (*JD*, 127). Marley's emphasis on Africa is romanticized, says Beckford, but it points the way for a reappropriation of an African heritage. In Marley, the church is reminded of the importance of revelation in music and in music making. Beckford acknowledges that Marley was fundamentally anti-Christian and saw Christianity as part of white oppression. Yet he sees Marley and Rastafarianism as addressing vital issues in the black community, which also need to be incorporated into the theology and practice of the church. Beckford's work draws on cultural studies to generate theological insights in popular culture, and as such it illustrates how the interests and concerns of practical theology are being worked out in dialogue with the social sciences.

## Culture and the Convergence of Academic Disciplines

The openness to practice in the study of religion and theology has arisen from a significant convergence of interests and approaches around the central importance of culture, community, and embodiment across the disciplines. Theologian Kathryn Tanner has spoken of the central importance of the category of culture across academic disciplines. Culture, she said, is a fundamental explanatory category, and it can be likened to gravity in physics, disease in medicine, and evolution in biology.[15] Culture introduces notions of the embodied and the lived across disciplines in the social sciences and in the arts and humanities. The effect of this is that there are common interests, concerns, analytical frameworks, and

15. Tanner, *Theories of Culture*, ix.

methods—inquiry that can be seen across a range of academic disciplines. Culture is a transforming idea that brings in new perspectives and changes the way that academic research takes place.

This cultural turn is also evident in the theological disciplines, and this more general move has produced a convergence around practice. The convergence around culture and the focus on practice has meant that, at times, it is hard to distinguish between academic disciplines in the study of religion because they are increasingly focusing on similar concerns and are using similar methods of study. This is an important insight in thinking about practical theology as it is done in relation to different academic disciplines. One consequence is that it is no longer possible to see practical theology as unique in the focus on practice because this perspective is shared across a range of disciplines.

This is a challenge, but it is also an exciting opportunity for the discipline because it now shares significant common ground with a range of different scholars and disciplines. In the next chapter, these insights are taken further by examining the interest in culture and contextualization in mission studies and liberation theology.

# 8

# Practical Theology as a Conversation about Culture

The practice of faith always takes place in a cultural context. Culture is therefore a key issue in practical theology. In fact, "culture" as category has been central to a wide range of debate and concern. In practical theology, questions of culture are crucial in several fields of discussion. Questions about, for instance, the future shape of the church, the character of Christian worship, the Christian education of children and young people, theology and social justice, or the public expression of faith all revolve around particular understandings of culture. In fact, it is hard to imagine any discussion of community and values without various understandings of culture playing some role. As a result, issues around culture and context have become a central concern in practical theology.

The interest in culture and contextualization is shared across a range of theological disciplines. This chapter draws on mission studies, and it gives an introduction to theories of culture and how context influences theology. Mission studies is discussed because it takes seriously both theology and practice. In other words, in my view it is very much part of the wider conversation that can be called "practical theology." So this chapter builds on the idea that what we regard as practical theology needs to be inclusive of a range of different fields in theological writing and research.

## Translation and Anthropological Notions of Culture

The development of "culture" as a category is closely linked to the emergence of anthropology as an academic discipline. In the nineteenth century, anthropologist Edward Burnett Tylor set out what has become a classic definition: "Culture or civilization, taken in its wide ethnographic sense, is that complex whole which includes knowledge, belief, art, morals, law, custom and any other capabilities and habits acquired by man as a member of society."[1] Tylor's definition reflects the way that anthropology has tended to see culture as a human universal and the "defining mark of human life."[2] In addition to seeing culture as universal, early anthropological views of culture also highlight its diversity. Different people or people groups are regarded as having different cultures. So culture is universal, and yet it is also plural.[3] Culture is both made by groups and also forms individuals into a group.[4]

Early anthropological ideas of culture have had a deep and enduring influence on the life of the church and on theology. The idea, for instance, that culture is a characteristic of distinct people groups and ethnicities has led to a sustained conversation about theological communication across and between cultures. Central to much of this discussion has been the idea of translation. Translation at its most simple expresses the idea that as faith moves between cultures, the gospel message can be reexpressed or translated. Translation obviously relates to the translation of language, but it is used here in a metaphorical way to relate to cultural reexpression or faith transmission between different cultural worlds or frameworks of expression.

Missiologist Lamin Sanneh suggests that translation was a fundamental characteristic of the early church. He argues that translation is clearly evident in the New Testament as the Christian message moves from a primarily Jewish context into the wider Hellenistic world. In the Acts of the Apostles and in the Letters, particularly in Galatians, the dilemma facing the leaders of the church centers on issues of culture and difference. Sanneh explains that the disciples and those who joined the group following the events of Pentecost were Jews; they worshiped in the temple, they continued to follow the law, and they circumcised their male children.

1. Tylor, *Primitive Culture*, 1, quoted in Jenks, *Culture*, 32–33.
2. Tanner, *Theories of Culture*, 25.
3. Ibid., 26.
4. Ibid., 28.

With the mission to the gentiles, questions were raised about the extent to which followers of Jesus who were not Jews should be expected to take on the Jewish religion as they accepted Christ. This dilemma brought about significant theological and cultural tension for the apostle Paul. The breakthrough in the mission to the gentiles brought Paul into a profound conflict with his cultural and religious assumptions. The result was that he was forced to question any claims for cultural absolutism based on his religious background.[5] Sanneh argues that this tension seen in the biblical account of the ministry of the apostle Paul is replicated in the experience of mission in the modern era. "As missionaries of the modern era were to find, encountering the reality of God beyond the inherited terms of one's culture reduces reliance on that culture as a universal normative pattern. A fresh standard of discernment is introduced by which the essence of the gospel is unscrambled from one cultural yoke in order to take firm hold in a different culture."[6]

Contrary to common wisdom, missionaries of the nineteenth and early twentieth centuries were not cultural imperialists, says Sanneh. In fact, their experience of traveling and living in different cultures meant that they often became advocates of translation and, consequently, spent a good deal of their time researching languages and indigenous cultural sources. The result was a concern for "the vernacular." The local dialect and expression in language became central to the missionary project. Through processes of translation, the Christian faith was able to find a place in the vernacular expression and cultural environments of the known world.[7]

Vincent Donovan's *Christianity Rediscovered: An Epistle from the Masai* illustrates how ideas of translation have been explored in mission studies. The book tells the story of Donovan, a Roman Catholic priest who went as a missionary to East Africa in 1955. When he arrived in Africa, Donovan found that the mission approach of the Roman Catholic Church was focused on developing institutions such as hospitals and schools. These were generally located in what were called mission compounds. The expectation was that evangelization would take place as the local Masai people came to access these services.

5. Sanneh, *Translating the Message*, 24.
6. Ibid., 25.
7. Ibid., 3.

Donovan soon became frustrated with this approach. He saw that, while people came for their medical treatment or for the schools, only a very small number found faith this way. He records how he began to talk with some of the Masai elders and asked them their perception of the Catholic mission. What he heard amazed him. The Masai he spoke to were quite puzzled. They had never realized that the intention of the missionaries was to share a message about God! They asked Donovan, "If that was your intention why did you never tell us that message?"[8]

The response of the young priest was at once rebellious and iconoclastic. He left the compound and set out on a series of journeys to visit Masai tribes in their villages. He began to sit with the tribal elders around their fires and tell them about Jesus and the gospel message. Storytelling lay at the heart of his approach, but he very soon realized that in order for the stories to make sense they had to be reformulated so that they took place in an environment and according to a logic that made sense for the Masai people. This meant that he had to translate the stories into the thought forms and cultural understanding of these nomadic African tribespeople.

Sitting down to tell the gospel story with the Masai immediately led Donovan to theological questions and problems. His assumption when he started to speak with his audience was that it was necessary to understand the concept of sin to apprehend the gospel. Donovan had learned that Jesus is the redeemer of the world and that redemption is necessary as a consequence of human sin. So Donovan introduced the story of Adam and Eve and the garden of Eden, the apple, the serpent, and the fall. He found that the people had their own stories of the fall, but these stories did not lead to any kind of similar consciousness of guilt, and therefore there was no sense of a need for a redeemer. So while he could tell the story, the way that his audience interpreted it was very different from what might be the case in, say, an American high school.

At the same time, the character of Adam and his location in a garden led these nomadic people to regard him as a kind of uncultured barbarian. "The Masai complained, with some justification, that our story about the beginning of the human race is more than a bit agriculturally biased, what with the garden and the fruit trees and the command to till the soil. For them, the cowboys of East Africa, tilling the soil is anathema. Only

8. Donovan, *Christianity Rediscovered*, 22.

an *olmeg* (a farmer, a barbarian) would cut open the thin layer of topsoil nurturing the life-giving grass of the Masai steppes, exposing it to the merciless equatorial sun, and turning it into desert within years."[9]

Donovan struggled to convince his listeners of universal sin based on the stories from Genesis, but his breakthrough came when a man asked him, "Can you forgive sin?" On investigation, it became clear that this man had committed a grave offense against someone in the tribe, and as a result he was shunned with no possibility of forgiveness. As Donovan explored the nature of sin among the Masai, he learned that it was seen primarily in relational terms. So if a son offended his father, he was deemed to have sinned and would have to work to provide recompense. Sin was a disruption of relationship. Reconciliation was symbolized through the use of spittle. The son would have to ask for the "spittle of forgiveness." Spittle was not just a symbol but also a sign that brought about forgiveness.[10]

For Donovan the rituals that connected forgiveness and the spittle of the father provided a set of symbolic concepts that enabled a "translation" of the Christian message of forgiveness into the symbolic world of the Masai. With this vital insight, Donovan explains how he proceeded to reexpress the Christian message in the thought forms of the Masai through the use of Bible stories that are relocated in an African world.

## Contextualization and Local Theology

Culture inevitably brings with it questions of power. In the Christian community, issues of culture and power have been clustered around the idea of context and contextualization. Catholic missiologist Stephen Bevans makes this point very powerfully. "There is no such thing as 'theology'; there is only *contextual* theology: *feminist* theology, *black* theology, *Filipino* theology, *Asian-American* theology, *African* theology and so forth."[11] The point is that cultural interest and perspectives inevitably shape theological expression. Power and cultural identity, says Bevans, are therefore inseparable from talk about God.

Catholic theologian Robert Schreiter describes contextual theology in terms that are very close to Sanneh's: as "local theology." Local theology,

9. Ibid., 57.
10. Ibid., 59.
11. Bevans, *Models of Contextual Theology*, 3.

he argues, has three main roots: gospel, culture, and the church. The gospel, says Schreiter, refers to the goodness of Jesus Christ and the salvation he has brought. This gospel, however, is not confined to a "message." It exists in an embodied form in the praxis of the local community. "It includes the Word that missionaries find already active in the culture upon their arrival. It refers to the living presence of the saving Lord that is the foundation of the community, the spirit of the risen Lord guiding that community, the prophetic Spirit challenging the culture and the larger church."[12] The gospel does not arrive in a vacuum, as if it had fallen from the sky. It is always incarnated in the lives and the communities of those who bring it to us. This is the church, a rich mixture of culture and presence in a local context. "Church is a complex of those cultural patterns in which the gospel has taken on flesh, at once enmeshed in the local situation, extending through communities in our own time and in the past, and reaching out to the eschatological realization of the fullness of God's reign."[13]

Culture is the actual setting within which all of these connections take place. It is the concrete reality in which there is a way of life with the associated values, symbols, and meanings. Local theology develops out of the dynamic interaction between these three elements. Local theology, Schreiter argues, should not be seen as a radical innovation in the life of the church. Contextualization has been a characteristic of theological creativity in every period. So from the perspective of contextualization, Christian tradition itself can be seen as a series of local theologies that have grown up to address the needs in particular contexts.[14]

Tradition viewed as a series of local theologies, then, becomes a source to aid the development of contextualized theologies in the present. Tradition gives validity and precedence for the construction of local theologies in contemporary contexts. At the same time, the residue of former local theologies also serves as a reference point and a corrective to inappropriate innovation.

The idea of theology as a local construct has been very influential in practical theology. An example of this is Laurie Green's pioneering work *Let's Do Theology*. Green situates theology in the ordinary expressions of individuals and communities. He challenges the prevailing idea that

12. Schreiter, *Constructing Local Theologies*, 21.
13. Ibid.
14. Ibid., 32.

theology is simply to be found in books and argues for theology as something that is present in the everyday experiences and choices of Christian people. Spiritual wisdom is not only to be found in theological texts; it is also carried in stories, proverbs, films, pop music, spirituals, poetry, handicrafts, dress, and dance. These diverse forms may be a place where the spiritual experiences of those who are not particularly "enamored of the chapel or the classroom" are discovered.[15]

Theology should never be the sole preserve of the trained academic. Every Christian, says Green, is a theologian. Some Christians, he admits, might be a little reluctant to embrace the idea that they are theologians, but all human beings are graced with the desire to make sense of life and of the world around them. So if theology is faith seeking understanding, then Christians will inevitably try to make sense of their own faith, and as they do so, they are being theologians.

Making sense can actually be an urgent necessity for believers as they are called to respond to a particular problem or situation.[16] In fact, theology should not be seen as a disinterested pursuit of knowledge. Rather, it is a calling to seek the transformation of the world and creation so that "people and society may conform through peace and justice to the Kingdom of God as inaugurated by Jesus Christ."[17] To do this, theologians cannot be detached from life; rather, they need to be involved on the ground working for the kingdom. For Green, theology is something that takes place in the context of ordinary life and ministry. It is local and contextual and emerges through the practice of faith. Doing theology involves a reflective engagement with action.

## Cultural Change and Reimagining Church

Alongside contextual forms of theology, the significance of culture and cultural change for the future shape of the church has seen an explosion of interest. Two missiologists, Lesslie Newbigin and David Bosch, have been at the heart of these developments. Both draw on culture in relation to mission, and both have been deeply significant for practitioners and those concerned with the theology of the church.

15. Green, *Let's Do Theology*, 6.
16. Ibid., 8.
17. Ibid., 12.

In the 1980s, missionary bishop and ecumenical theologian Lesslie
Newbigin developed a missiological ecclesiology. Growing out of work
with the World Council of Churches, Newbigin wrote *The Other Side
of 1984.*[18] This book and a subsequent volume, *The Gospel in a Pluralist Society*, published in 1989, eventually led to the launch of the gospel
and culture movement.[19] In his writing, Newbigin uses insights from
missiology to develop a perspective on what he calls "modern Western
culture."[20] His starting point is the assertion that the contemporary
church has experienced a weakening of confidence in inherited expressions of the faith. As a result, says Newbigin, Christians have become
aware of the extent to which in sharing faith they have "often confused
culturally conditioned perceptions with the substance of the gospel" (*FG*,
2). He embraces the idea of contextualization within missiology, yet he
is critical of the way that the literature in mission studies has failed to
deal with the culture from which this work is generated (i.e., modern
Western culture; *FG*, 3).

Newbigin adopts anthropological understandings of culture. Culture,
he says, is "the sum total of ways of living developed by a group of human
beings and handed on from generation to generation." Language is central to the notion of culture, and around this center are grouped artistic,
technological, and political ways of organizing. Fundamental to culture
are the beliefs, experiences, and practices "that seek to grasp and express
the ultimate nature of things." These act together to give meaning to life,
and they claim a "final loyalty." This latter area Newbigin identifies as the
place of religion in culture (*FG*, 3). For Newbigin, the life, ministry, death,
and resurrection of Jesus Christ shape the gospel, but the gospel is always
expressed in culture. Yet while it is cultural in its form of expression, the
gospel also calls every human culture to account (*FG*, 4). So the gospel
must be shared within the thought forms of the culture within which it is
communicated, but as it is communicated it should also offer a critique
of that culture (*FG*, 5–6).

Newbigin's specific critique of Western Christianity is that it is guilty
of syncretism (*FG*, 9). He perceives the church to have imported an alien
understanding of faith in relation to the private and personal spheres.

18. Newbigin, *Other Side of 1984.*
19. Weston, *Lesslie Newbigin, Missionary Theologian*, 13.
20. Newbigin, *Foolishness to the Greeks*, 1 (hereafter cited in text as *FG*).

This, he says, is the "operative plausibility structure of the modern world" (*FG*, 14). He makes the link between this plausibility structure and what he terms the dominant Western scientific worldview (*FG*, 15). He traces the roots between this worldview and the effects of the Enlightenment, in particular Kantian metaphysics (*FG*, 25). While he deals with these developments primarily in terms of the history of ideas, he makes the point that these ideas function as a way of life. As Newbigin puts it, "Plainly what we call modern Western culture is much more than a body of ideas. It is a whole way of organizing human life that both rests on and in turn supports and validates the ideas" (*FG*, 29).

Newbigin launches an assault on those developments in the Western church that he regards as being an abandonment of the public nature of belief and in response argues that the gospel itself offers an alternative plausibility structure. It is not possible, he says, to argue rationally for this position; rather, this is a matter of costly obedience and faithfulness on the part of Christian people. The missional approach to Western culture will "call for radical conversion." "This will be not only a conversion of the will and of the feelings but a conversion of the mind—a 'paradigm shift' that leads to a new vision of how things are." The result will be the development of a new plausibility structure in which "the most real of all realities is the living God whose character is 'rendered' for us in the pages of Scripture" (*FG*, 64).

Paradigm shifts lie at the heart of David Bosch's work. Like Newbigin, Bosch suggests that changes in the church and theology come about in response to cultural change. For Bosch, however, the present response to culture forms part of a larger pattern of paradigm shifts in Christian history. In *Transforming Mission*, published in 1992, he sets out to describe Christian history in six different epochs, each with its own distinctive theological paradigm: the apocalyptic paradigm of primitive Christianity, the Hellenistic paradigm of the patristic era, the medieval Roman Catholic paradigm, the Protestant (Reformation) paradigm, the modern Enlightenment paradigm, and the emerging ecumenical paradigm.[21]

Bosch derives the idea of paradigm shifts from Thomas Kuhn's *The Structure of Scientific Revolutions*. Kuhn argues that rather than progressing gradually and incrementally, science moves forward through a series

21. Bosch, *Transforming Mission*, 185.

of radical disruptions in the framework of knowledge. His term for a change in the framework of knowledge is a paradigm shift. Drawing on Kuhn, Hans Küng and David Tracy identified a series of different eras or paradigms in theology. "In each era the Christians of that period understood and experienced their faith in ways only partially commensurable with the understanding and experience of believers of the other eras."[22] Bosch took Küng and Tracy's understanding that there were different eras in theology where distinctive paradigms were dominant and applied it to the understanding of mission.

Fundamental to Bosch's argument is the assertion that we are currently in the midst of a paradigm shift from the modern Enlightenment paradigm to a new paradigm. Yet whereas Bosch describes all earlier paradigms as coherent frameworks, he is unable to describe the present in a structured way. So the present day is discussed as a series of different and often conflicting developments and movements. These characterize what he calls the "emerging ecumenical missionary paradigm."[23] The emerging themes represent a particular revolution in the structure of knowledge shaped around the rejection of Enlightenment frameworks. So the modern is gradually being replaced by the postmodern.

Postmodern perspectives in theology have been quite widespread, but Bosch's work has been more influential than most because it makes an explicit link between issues of contextualization, the practice of mission, and ecclesiology. Bosch's work is important in practical theology because it connects theological change and cultural change. Most significantly, it introduced the notion of "emergence" into present-day debates around the future shape of the church. Bosch's work lies, for instance, behind the influential report by the Church of England, *Mission-Shaped Church*. The report echoes the idea of paradigm shifts when it argues that changes in culture necessitate new initiatives in mission and that mission in turn gives birth to new forms of ecclesiology. "We face a significant moment of opportunity. Western society has undergone a massive transition in recent decades. . . . The Church needs to respond to the changes in our culture. Thus it is important for us to see what our culture now looks like, so we can see the possible shape, or shapes, of church to which God is calling

22. See ibid., 187.
23. Ibid., 377.

us."[24] The argument that cultural change necessitates an ecclesial response has become central to much of the contemporary conversation around the future shape of the church.

## Practical Theology and Popular Culture

Contemporary definitions of culture tend to emphasize communication over earlier anthropological notions of culture as a characteristic of people groups. Culture is seen as fluid. Cultural forms shift and alter as people come into contact with one another. A good example of this is the British obsession with curry. Some popular polls indicate that it is no longer fish and chips or roast beef that is the national dish of the British but chicken tikka masala. Yet curry as we know it has only a slight relationship to what people cook and eat on the Indian subcontinent. The food we get in restaurants in the United Kingdom has developed over time in response to Western tastes. What we think of as Indian food in the West is therefore a conglomerate of different ingredients and ways of cooking that have developed to please the British palate. Interestingly, judging from the menus at my local restaurants, curry is now merging with different kinds of Thai and Nepalese dishes. So even something as basic to culture as food is increasingly part of the ebb and flow of global life.

The idea of communication treats culture as flows of interaction between individuals and groups. Central to this approach to culture is the role that institutions, such as the media, play in the circulation of different kinds of communication. So alongside more traditional structures such as family or ethnic group, businesses and media platforms serve as sites for cultural communication. In contemporary culture, it is argued, the sense of self is constructed in relation to media representation. This understanding of contemporary culture and identity construction has been particularly influential for practical theology. Youth ministry practitioners have for some time been aware of the ways in which young people build their particular taste cultures around music and fashion. Much of the church's work with young people in the United States and in the United Kingdom has been oriented around this basic insight. As a result, we have seen many contemporary churches being shaped around ways of

24. Archbishop's Council, *Mission-Shaped Church*, 1.

communicating and associating that come from youth culture. In *Growing Up Evangelical* I trace the way evangelical Anglicans developed their distinctive style of expression and church life based on ministry among young people and students. What worked on the university campus was eventually imported into church.

In *Understanding Theology and Popular Culture*, Gordon Lynch maps the various ways that academics in theology and religious studies have started to discuss contemporary forms of cultural expression. He identifies four different approaches. The first approach focuses on the study of religion in everyday life. In recent years, Lynch observes, there has been a shift in religious studies away from the study of religion as an abstract form toward the practice of faith in everyday life. A feature of this turn toward the lived has been an increasing interest in how communities and individuals construct faith in relation to the texts and the forms of communication that characterize popular culture. Examples of this might be the ways that contemporary Christian music draws on conventions and genres of popular music or the visual culture of Protestants and Catholics.[25] Religious groups in various ways have been shaped by their interaction with popular culture.

Alongside this, popular culture has also taken up religion and represented it in a variety of ways. The examination of religious themes in film, for instance, or in popular music, has been a fruitful area of research. For Lynch, analyzing the representation of religion in popular culture is not simply descriptive. "Rather it involves asking what these representations may tell us about wider biases, values, and concerns in contemporary society, what interests these representations might serve, and how these representations may be helpful or damaging to particular groups or individuals" (*UT*, 24). Religious communities have often sought to interact with the media in various ways. This might include protests over the ways in which the media have portrayed religious figures, or it might be protests over the influence that Hollywood has on morality. These kinds of culture wars have become a feature of the everyday relationship between popular culture and religious groups (*UT*, 25).

Functionalist approaches to religion and popular culture form the second main approach identified by Lynch. This approach seeks to interpret

25. Lynch, *Understanding Theology*, 22 (hereafter cited in text as *UT*).

popular culture as in some way operating like religion. Central to these discussions are developments in the way religion is defined. Lynch draws in part on Paul Tillich's definition of religion as that which is of ultimate concern. So if religion is the search for what forms people's ultimate concern, then these wishes are often observed within cultural expression. Tillich was dismissive of popular culture, but in recent years the attention of scholars has increasingly been drawn toward the ways in which contemporary music, sports, or film exhibit the ultimate concerns of many people.

The forms of popular culture have been seen as functioning like religion in three main ways. The first, says Lynch, relates to the social function of religion. An example of this is the interpretation of sports as religion. Here sporting events are seen as groups gathering together, the rituals of fan behavior are seen as being parallel to religious practice, and sports stars are regarded as operating as iconic figures (*UT*, 30). The second relates to the way popular culture helps to offer categories and metaphors for understanding life and how these are taken up by individuals and groups in meaning making. Lynch terms this the existential/hermeneutical function of popular culture. An example of this might be the way that films draw people into an alternative world that serves to frame key issues, such as sex and relationships or power and communities, in novel forms. "Films can be understood as offering images of what it means to live the good life, or to act virtuously, that can act as a resource for our own everyday reflections on how we should live" (*UT*, 31). Finally, some scholars see popular culture as an arena within which people may experience the transcendent. An example of this is work on rave and dance culture that explores the extent to which through communal behavior (the sonic landscapes created by dance music and drug taking) participants might be drawn into religious experience (*UT*, 33).

Popular culture has been an emerging concern within the whole area of missiology. The conviction that cultural change (and popular culture in particular) forms a new and challenging environment for the expression of faith and the life of the church has led to a range of different studies in theology and popular culture. This is the third approach that Lynch identifies. These studies, he says, fall into two main groups. First, there are those treatments of popular culture that seek to emphasize the limitations and the problems with popular culture. These works tend to contrast Christian faith and the life of the church with what is perceived as the more profane arena of the popular. Other studies are more positive about the religious and theological significance of popular culture. Approaches in this second group seek to construct theologies that learn from and build upon popular culture. This move toward the popular is seen as a missiological imperative. So it might be argued that in order to connect to the lives of young people, it is vital that the church makes use of the forms of communication. In particular, music plays an important role in youth cultures.

Alongside the negative and the more affirming approaches to popular culture, there are a growing number of studies that seek to reflect theologically on the texts and practices of popular culture. This is the fourth approach to theology and popular culture that Lynch describes. An example of this is the now well-established body of work that discusses theology and film; scholars have sought to discuss theological themes through both the texts of films and also through the more traditional theological resources of the Scriptures or of systematic theology. This kind of work emphasizes the importance of dialogue and, in particular, of ways in which theologians position themselves in relation to the texts of film as empathetic viewers. So this approach rests on the conviction that a text or a practice from popular culture should be "taken seriously on its own terms (i.e., its own 'voice' needs to be heard) in order for a proper conversation between theology and popular culture to take place" (*UT*, 37).

## The Irreverent Spirituality of Generation X

Interest in popular culture has led some practical theologians to consider the extent to which those outside the church share a theological perspective. One of the pioneers in this kind of practical theology is practical theologian Tom Beaudoin. *Virtual Faith: The Irreverent Spiritual Quest of Generation X*, when it was published in 1998, was a groundbreaking attempt to express the extent to which popular culture revealed a theology that operated at a popular level. Beaudoin analyzed the content of films, music, music videos, and rock concerts to develop an understanding of spirituality in contemporary culture. His assertion is that the young people who make up Generation X (i.e., those born in the 1960s and '70s) are strikingly religious, but their spirituality does not conform to traditional understandings of spirituality or religion.

By observing the expression of spirituality in popular cultural forms, he developed "Generation X theology." This is a theology constructed "*by, for,* and *about* Generation X."[26] He calls his work a theological interpretation of Generation X culture. "It is theological because it is concerned with the religiousness of a generation and its culture. Its object is GenX pop culture because that is where I think Generation X has implicitly displayed its lived theology for at least the past two decades of its young life."[27]

Based on his research, Beaudoin developed a practical theology that he sees as both actual and potential, meaning that it is lived and is also yet to be explored. This theology relates to four key themes. First, Generation X has a deep suspicion of religious institutions. It has an antipathy to churches, and this suspicion is particularly directed toward the Roman Catholic Church. Generation X frequently opposes Jesus and the perceived inadequacies of the church. The second theme is an emphasis on the sacred nature of experience. Pop culture, says Beaudoin, "often features experiences that fuse either the human and the divine or the sensual and the spiritual."[28] The third theme centers on pop culture's focus on how this particular generation has suffered. There is an interest in the significance of figures that endure suffering, and at the same time there is a tendency to see history and politics through a prophetic gaze that predicts a final dramatic conflagration. These three themes are brought together in the fourth, what he calls a "meta theme" of virtual reality. There is an overarching sense in which, through popular culture, Generation X imitates what it is to be religious. He calls this "religiosity" because the term includes not only the practice of religion but also the suggestion that such practice might be manufactured in some way. "Religiosity is the perfect word for the sort of authentic and fake, real and unreal religious practice that much of Generation X popular culture indicates."[29]

## The Problem of Taste in Practical Theology

The widespread move to embrace contemporary culture in the church has not been without its critics. Theologians have for some years been uneasy

26. Beaudoin, *Virtual Faith*, xiv.
27. Ibid., xvii.
28. Ibid., 41.
29. Ibid., 42.

about the influence of popular culture in society as well as in the church. Paul Tillich, for instance, was highly dismissive of popular culture. As we saw in chapter 5, Tillich is seen in practical theology as the architect of correlation. The method advocates a theological openness to the questions of wider society. Yet for Tillich this openness never included popular forms of expression.

Tillich was deeply influenced by his fellow German migrant to the United States, Theodor Adorno. Adorno argued that popular culture is the unfortunate product of industrial processes of "standardization." Standardization, he said, produces patterned and unimaginative cultural products that satisfy the lowest common denominator in the consumer. Workers on the factory line or in offices demand entertainment. They seek novelty, but they do so, argues Adorno, with an inability to make any effort. Workers seek "effortless sensation."[30] Writing in 1945, Tillich identified mass communication as a significant factor in the conflagration that took place in Nazi Germany leading to the Second World War. Standardized communication, he argued, "through the radio, movies, press, and fashions tends to create standardized men who are all too susceptible to propaganda for old or new totalitarian purposes."[31]

Current political concerns may have moved beyond those of Tillich and Adorno, but it is still common to hear similar views about popular culture. Popular culture is often characterized as being substandard and shallow and is dismissed as "consumerism." In contrast, the theology and the culture of the church is often presented as a deeper, more authentic alternative to a distracting, media-obsessed world. The problem with these kinds of judgments is that it is often difficult to distinguish theological statements from issues of taste. Taste as a concept relates closely to one of the most influential and persistent ways of talking about culture as a comparison between high forms and low forms of cultural expression.

The earliest use of the word "culture" comes from farming. To culture something was to grow it. For something to be cultured meant that it had been grown in the right way. From this notion of culture, it was a short step to talking about education as a form of culturing. To be well educated was to be a "cultured" person. Culture then shifts from a process to the

30. Quoted in Storey, *Cultural Theory and Popular Culture*, 211.
31. Quoted in Cobb, *Blackwell Guide to Theology and Popular Culture*, 98.

content of education. Culture becomes right kinds of materials that will shape the mind in the right way.[32]

Central to the notion of culture as the right way of educating has been a distinction between high forms and low forms of cultural expression. High culture is that which makes someone into a "cultured" person (i.e., one who has been educated in the right way). Low culture is everything else. Low culture therefore becomes inseparable from the forms of expression shared by the masses. The classic expression of this position comes in the nineteenth century from the English educationalist Matthew Arnold, who describes culture as the best knowledge and the best ideas. Those who oppose the "sweetness and light" that leads to perfection are "Philistines and Barbarians," and the only defense against their malign influence is education. Culture was, for Arnold, about the perfecting of human nature, and one of the chief means whereby this perfection was developed was through Christianity and the practice and doctrine of the Anglican Church in particular.[33]

The thinking of Arnold still casts a long shadow over the church and the wider culture. It is hard, for instance, to talk about the visual arts, classical music, or theater without importing some notion that these are more worthy or more profound forms of expression than football, pop music, or video games. Our thinking is structured around a divide between high culture and low culture. Bishop Richard Holloway, the former Anglican primate of Scotland, once said that the distinguishing feature of evangelical Christianity is that it is willing to embrace "bad taste" in the service of the gospel. Holloway calls this a "courageous act," as if for him such a sacrifice would be unthinkable![34] This kind of cultural snobbery is thankfully not too common in church life, but nevertheless there remain many who have a strong conviction that particular kinds of Christian worship are "improving" and part of a more valuable cultural residue than the "ephemera" of popular culture.

The besetting problem with ideas of high culture and low culture is that they seem to rest on social- and class-based distinctions. Arnold's notion of the best ideas for the best "men" was closely allied to forms of private education that fostered and maintained privilege. The shift toward

32. Raymond Williams, *Culture*, 10.
33. Arnold, *Culture and Anarchy*.
34. France and McGrath, *Evangelical Anglicans*, 182.

a Christianity and a church shaped by an engagement with contemporary forms of expression is a deliberate attempt to unhook church culture from structures of privilege. There is then a direct connection between the development of contextual forms of theology and developments in new forms of ecclesiology in the West. At the same time, whereas contextual theology has sought to foreground issues of power by seeking the voices of, for instance, women or African Americans or particular groups who are poor or disadvantaged, ecclesiologies rooted in popular culture are often less concerned with these issues.

One of the reasons for the frequent failure to engage with power and disadvantage comes from how culture is understood. For liberation theology, power is structured around oppositions. The origins of this lie in Marxism, in which culture is understood in terms of a struggle between those who own the means of production and those who do not. A similar structuring of issues of power lies behind feminist theology and black theology. When culture is seen as communication, questions of power are made more fluid and less easy to identify and define. This is what sociologist Zygmunt Bauman calls "liquid modernity": an arena where solid social structures become fluid and we are subject to constant change. In this liquid culture, taste does not disappear—it becomes more significant because individuals seek places where they can build communities of refuge and sanctuary to survive the deluge. So the fluidity of cultural change leads to the solidifying of voluntary institutions, such as churches, as they reconstitute themselves around the need for significance and survival. There is, therefore, something of a catch-22 situation here for the church. As it seeks to make meaning in the wider popular culture, it is always in danger of simultaneously closing itself off, which is driven by the needs and anxieties of its members.

## Culture in Practical Theology: What Is at Stake

One of the characteristics of culture is that it comes naturally to us. Just by being human, we share in cultural norms and values. Dominant cultural patterns often operate below the surface. We are not always aware of their influence. Sanneh's discussion of the way that mission across cultures affects missionaries is instructive at this point. Exposure to different societies and communities through, for instance, an extended period working overseas often leads to a heightened awareness of the ways in which someone has been shaped and formed by their own cultural background. In previous centuries, this kind of cross-cultural exposure was common, but it took place in a much more defined and clear way. Africa or India was a long boat journey away. Home and overseas were obviously delineated. Globalization has swept these well-marked differences away. Cities such as London and New York and Paris, but also many smaller cities, are now multicultural. It is not at all uncommon in these places to find churches that have people from four or five or more "cultures" present every Sunday. In these circumstances, we do not have the luxury of culture being separated by a long boat journey. Translation is no longer a binary process of trying to communicate from one cultural and linguistic framework to another.

A similar point can be made about contextualization. In globalization there is no longer one context to learn, but many. Issues of power and privilege have of course not gone away; they are just more difficult to identify. Fluidity makes them more slippery. So, for instance, the recent crises in finance and banking are rather resistant to clear analysis. There seem to be winners and losers, rich and poor, but developing a constructive and critical theological response, while it is necessary, is more complex when we cannot distinguish with any conviction who precisely is "us" and "them."

Lesslie Newbigin is clear about the challenges posed by culture. Faith, he says, must be expressed within culture. Churches are cultural constructs, but the gospel of Jesus Christ should never be so closely identified with particular kinds of cultural expression that it becomes unable to call a culture to account. This call for a return to "theology" echoes the work of Thomas Oden and Ray Anderson that we saw in chapter 5. The problem with this appeal to theology is that it tends to locate theology as something outside cultural expression. The opposite move locates theology as part of the expression of the church. Questions of authority or normativity are then located as part of the conversation in the church. One of the problems with this position is that it fails to make allowance for the ways in which, as Christian communities engage in everyday practices of worship and daily living, the Scriptures and the tradition of the church call the community to account. This calling to account is seen as something that comes from outside. It is the prompting of the Spirit, the stirring of the prophetic, and the call of Jesus Christ. It is possible to see these processes at work in a community through different kinds of observation and research drawn from the social sciences. The voice of God is evident in the practices of communities. The presence of Christ in the church takes a cultural form, but it should not be reduced to the cultural.

This brief treatment of questions of culture has shown how fundamental culture has become in all kinds of theology. Practical theology is therefore not alone in being interested in questions of contextualization, cultural transmission, and power. These issues have come right to the foreground in any kind of practical theological work, but as with anything important, they have become a contentious area, and there are different schools of thought and ways of dealing with these questions. This chapter has mapped some of these issues and shown what may or may not be at stake in this conversation. In the final two chapters I move from theoretical frameworks to the more hands-on work of actually doing practical theology. Chapter 9 looks at doing empirical research as part of practical theology, and chapter 10 discusses the eventual results or outputs that come from doing practical theology.

# 9

# Beginning Small-Scale Empirical Research

I am here among these working-class people in this postindustrial landscape because I want to hear their stories. I take their voices seriously. This is what research in religion means, I fume, to attend to the experiences and beliefs of people in the midst of their lives, to encounter religion in its place in actual men and women's lived experience, in the places where they live and work. Where are the theologians from the seminaries on the South Side, I want to know, with all their talk of postmodernism and narrativity? When will the study of religion in the United States take an empirical and so more realistic and humane direction?

—Robert Orsi, *Between Heaven and Earth*

Robert Orsi's impassioned plea for theology and religious studies to start to pay attention to the rich and detailed religious experience of communities has inspired me for some time now. The criticism of theologians is stinging. Orsi's reference to the "South Side" comes from his location in Chicago when he was doing this research. The South Side is code for the Catholic liberation theologians who were so prominent in Chicago at the time. Orsi is pointing out that even these contextual theologians appeared to not be concerned with the lives of ordinary Catholics. It is this critique and others like it that anyone doing practical theology needs to heed. Paying attention is something that we do not simply because the pastoral cycle says that we should or because the course we are studying demands it. Paying attention, and by this Orsi means spending time getting to know communities and people by being with them and walking for a while in their shoes, is a moral and ethical calling. In fact, I would say it is a theological calling.

## Empirical Research and the Love of Christ

The Byzantine theologian Nicholas Cabasilas describes the love of Jesus Christ as *manikos eros*. This can be translated as passionate, mad, or crazy love. Cabasilas likens Jesus Christ to someone caught up in the first phases of a love affair, unable to resist just being near the person he has become obsessed with.[1] The same is true of the way that, out of crazy love, Jesus Christ is drawn to human beings. He is willing to wait outside the door hoping to be invited in. His love is such that he is willing to be ignored or rejected and even to be killed. This is the love that the church experiences in the Eucharist: the presence of Christ, love offered freely on the cross and in the bread and the wine simply because of love.

It is this experience of Christ that should fuel a theological approach to empirical research. Practical theologian Richard Osmer likens the practice of empirical research to the way that ministers in churches have a responsibility to pay attention to their congregation and to communities. He calls this a kind of "priestly listening."[2] Listening can be sacramental and formal, or it can simply be the prayerful intention to be present and open in a community. This kind of listening, however, should not be seen just as a technique of ministry or a professional way of operating in a community. Listening and presence, I would argue, have their origins in the love of Jesus Christ.

Listening and paying attention to Christian communities and to the wider society is a practice not simply of the minister but of all Christians. Paying attention is part of the call to pray for the world and for the church. The link to empirical research, however, is that this everyday practice can

1. Cabasilas, *Life in Christ*, 162–63.
2. Osmer, *Practical Theology*, 35.

be sharpened and given tools that make it more precise or intentioned. Empirical research, then, can be seen as simply a more developed way of practicing a ministry that is part of the everyday lives of Christians.

Osmer suggests a "continuum of attending," with ministerial and inter-personal listening at one end; he calls this informal attending. He places academically funded empirical research projects at the other end of the continuum; this academic work he calls formal attending. Formal attend-ing includes using the academic research of other people or developing your own research. Between informal and formal attending are different kinds of small-scale research and attentiveness, which Osmer calls semi-formal.[3] This chapter will focus on the sorts of semiformal empirical research that can be undertaken as part of ministerial training or everyday practice.

## Theology and Empirical Research

The idea of informal attending or listening is a reminder that Christian believers and ministers already do a kind of empirical research by being faithful and present and by paying attention. Semiformal or more struc-tured ways of paying attention can help in theological reflection on minis-try and practice. Empirical research brings something unique and special to the theological table: it enables theologians to investigate present-day practice and experience. An empirical project might take different forms, including exploring the self, exploring the community, testing theological assertions, testing ecclesial assertions, generating new theological perspec-tives, or correcting problems.

### Exploring the Self

Empirical research can help theologians focus on individuals. This might start with our own selves. Keeping a journal and reviewing what you write on a regular basis can be a very simple way of reflecting on the Chris-tian life. This kind of writing practice could become more focused and intentional. One idea for a small-scale research project is to keep a diary of your daily prayer life. The diary doesn't need to be written down. You could use your phone to record your thoughts throughout the day. Your

3. Ibid., 37–39.

prayer diary could be a record of when and indeed if you have prayed. It could also include notes on what prompted that prayer, and you could write out some of the prayers that you have used. After a few weeks, you could set aside some time to analyze what you have written. The point here is to look for repeated patterns or particularly striking examples. How we pray not only reveals what we are worried about or concerned with but also says a great deal about how we think about God and how God works in the world.

### Exploring the Community

Small-scale research is an ideal way to begin to research communities. Christian communities share a common life as they participate together in worship and social action. There are theological differences between communities and also within communities. Small-scale research projects are a way for practical theologians to investigate aspects of the life of a community. This can lead to a theological evaluation of the strengths and the possible problems that might form part of the congregation's life.

Using prayer again as an example, one question might concern the kinds of prayer that shape the daily life of a community. In other words, while a congregation may share in a regular service, do its members have similar approaches to personal prayer, and what does their prayer say about the theological identity of the church? These kinds of questions could be investigated using the prayer diary method, but there will also need to be a time to gather this material together. One way to do this is to hold a small group meeting where individuals share their own prayer diaries with each other. This kind of activity could serve not simply as research but as a way to develop the prayer practices in a community. One further technique to share these experiences more widely might be to write a report about the prayer diaries and the group discussion to post on the church website or to make available in the church newsletter. This kind of reporting will raise some technical issues around informed consent and deciding whether those participating should be identified. I will discuss these concerns in more detail later in the chapter.

Closely linked to community, the idea of ordinary theology, introduced in chapter 4, also lends itself to this form of research. Small-scale projects are a way to investigate the kinds of theological expression and ways of acting and thinking that make up the everyday lives of communities. Ordinary theology is often difficult to uncover because it is so much a part of the way we live as Christians. Small-scale research can be a useful way of bringing it to our awareness.

## Types of Empirical Research

Empirical research divides into two main types: quantitative and qualitative. Quantitative research involves numbers. Without numbers, research is qualitative rather than quantitative.[4] Any data that requires counting something is quantitative. An example is a project that involves counting attendance at church or the numbers of people who read the Bible daily. This counting can be nuanced to make it possible, for instance, to examine Bible-reading habits by age group or by area.

A key part of the research design in quantitative research has to do with the sample. The reliability of a survey will depend on the extent to which the sample can be seen as representative of a wider group. Sampling is necessary because it is generally impossible to ensure the participation of everyone within a given group, so a smaller group that will be representative of the whole needs to be selected. In a congregation with a certain age, gender, and racial mix, for instance, the proportions of those selected for the sample should match the proportions in the larger congregational group. Another key to good surveys is making sure they are carefully designed in order to elicit accurate and reliable results and then to analyze these results using statistical methods.[5]

The primary focus of this chapter, however, will be qualitative research, since this type of research is most easily undertaken as a small-scale project and connects most readily to practical theology. While quantitative research makes numerical measurements, qualitative research explores the complexity and rich nature of experience. The aim of qualitative research is to generate an in-depth appreciation of social reality. This means that while quantitative research relies on samples and the statistical analysis of surveys, qualitative research has developed ways of examining particular cases or instances in detail. This enables the researcher to pay close

---

4. "Quantitative and Qualitative Research Methods," *Skills You Need*, http://www.skills youneed.com/learn/quantitative-and-qualitative.html.

5. For more on small-scale survey-based research, see Punch, *Survey Research*.

attention to what is happening and to examine their own reactions to what they are observing. In qualitative research, then, the researcher becomes the main tool for doing the research. David Silverman has identified four main methods for qualitative research: observation, analyzing texts and documents, interviewing, and recording and transcription.[6]

*Observation* involves paying attention. It is often referred to as participant observation. This acknowledges that researchers should not regard themselves as outside the social situation they are observing; rather, they are part of the action. A good example of this is the observation of a worship service in which a researcher joins in with the singing and the liturgy as part of the research process. What is being observed is not simply what is happening in the service but also what the researcher feels as she is singing, praying, or listening to the sermon. Observation is a good way to become aware of bodily gestures and the different ways that people interact with a situation. Again, in a worship service, observation might reveal how parents interact with their children during worship, how people sit in places out of habit, or how different people use their bodies when they are singing, some raising their hands and others swaying in time to the music. Observation is also a good way to clarify or confirm comments that are made in an interview. A youth minister, for instance, might tell a researcher that his congregation's young people enjoy the regular worship, but an observer might see the ways they mentally check out during a worship service—using their phones, whispering to each other, or just looking bored.

Qualitative research does not always involve working directly with communities and individuals. It can also involve *analyzing texts and documents*. In a church context a whole range of materials can reveal how the community works. One example is the church newsletter or magazine. Many churches produce a weekly or monthly newsletter. In more recent times these may have been replaced by a website, a Facebook page, or an email. One way of researching newsletters is to examine them over a period of time. One example is the minister who took up a new position in a church and decided to look through the cupboards in the church office. There she found newsletters and church attendance records that went back thirty or forty years. From this material she was able to generate a detailed account of the activities that shaped the life of the church over a period of time. Some

6. Silverman, *Interpreting Qualitative Data*, 9–11.

groups started up and then seemed to drift out of the record. The arrival of different clergy seemed to be marked by new initiatives and a change of tone in the messages written in the newsletters. By carefully reading through these, the cultural and theological history of the community could be observed.

One of the most common methods used in qualitative research is *interviewing*.[7] Interviews can take many different forms. Sometimes interviews are face-to-face with an individual, while at other times they are done with groups of people. The latter are sometimes called focus groups.[8] In qualitative research, interview questions are used as a way to shape a conversation, but the intention is for the conversation to develop and explore areas that are interesting. This kind of interviewing is called semi-structured because it starts with planned questions but is flexible and allows the interviewer and the person being interviewed to discuss whatever seems most interesting. The aim is to generate detailed and rich material rather than to simply answer questions that have been predetermined. This means that the interviewer needs to ask more open questions that facilitate complex answers as opposed to closed questions that tend to result in simple yes or no answers.

A key part of research will be the *recording and transcription* of interviews and field notes. Participant observation is generally undertaken using a simple form of note-taking. This can be in a notebook, or it could be speaking into a recording device such as a phone. Sometimes researchers will follow up their observation by writing down their impressions and thoughts. The purpose of this kind of recording is not simply to remember what has happened but to look for patterns in the observations and also in their own reaction to what has happened. These patterns may not at first be evident, so the recordings enable them to look back at what they have experienced and start to formulate an analysis. Sometimes observation is supported by the use of video. Viewing the event again can provide another level of observation.

## Being a Qualitative Researcher

Setting out to do qualitative research involves more than simply adopting some empirical methods. Qualitative research is based on a way of

7. For more on interviews in qualitative research, see Kvale, *InterViews*.
8. See Morgan, *Focus Groups as Qualitative Research*.

approaching the social world. It has values rooted in usual ways of observing and operating. Julie Scott Jones and Sal Watt summarize the core values of qualitative research as participation; immersion; reflection, reflexivity, and representation; thick description; an active participative ethics; and empowerment and understanding.[9]

*Participation* is not simply a method in qualitative research; it is also a value. Participation is built on the conviction that in order to know about people or communities, it is necessary to take the time to share in their lives. There are obvious links here with theological ideas of participation as relationship and the basis of knowing being a kind of sharing.

Similar themes are found in the second value described by Jones and Watt: *immersion*. Qualitative research is not about trying to be a detached or objective observer of people or society. Rather, this kind of research embraces the subject of the researcher as the chief means of getting at the detail of what is happening, and this requires the researcher to dive right in to the research. Sometimes this means spending long periods of time with a group, or spending time interacting with people online. If the research deals with printed material such as magazines or newsletters, then immersion is the discipline of allowing the material to speak. This again has echoes of theological notions of incarnation and presence.

The values of *reflection, reflexivity, and representation* also lie at the heart of this kind of research. The expectation is that researchers will be continually reflecting on their own experiences as they do the research and also on what they are discovering as they are conducting the project. This reflection means that methods, interview questions, and ways of analyzing and describing what is found will be reviewed, adjusted, and developed as the project progresses. "Reflexivity" is the technical term that researchers use to describe spending time thinking about how their own beliefs, background, and experiences help inform and shape the research. The purpose here is not to exclude or to try to minimize possible bias but to accept that sharing in a social situation and reflecting on ourselves in a context necessarily means that as researchers we need to write ourselves into the picture. This means that where we are coming from is set out and available to anyone reading the work. Again, this is intended as a way to embrace the position of researcher, and it is a rejection of forms of research that appear to be distanced

---

9. Jones and Watt, *Ethnography in Social Science Practice*, 7.

or objective. Representation refers to the act of writing and, in particular, attention to the way that people being researched are spoken about and represented. Qualitative research is therefore concerned to take seriously issues of inequality and power in writing about people and communities.

*Thick description* is a way of describing the kind of knowledge that qualitative researchers hope to generate. The intention is to try to offer an insight into the multilayered and rich nature of social life. We have already seen how practical theologians John Swinton and Harriet Mowat talk about qualitative research as a means to "complexify" situations.[10] What they mean is that this kind of research intends to get beneath the surface of things and to not accept uncritically what at first appears to be the case. This is why in analyzing recordings it is necessary to be immersed in the detail of the material to search for different levels of interpretation and understanding.

The value of *an active participative ethics* makes reference to the issues of power that come about in researching people and communities. This links closely to the question of representation already mentioned. Qualitative research is acutely aware that researchers in the past have written about communities from the position of Western and white. The net effect of this has been a kind of colonial "gaze" that positions cultures as uncivilized or exotic. Active participative ethics has arisen to combat these problems, and it encourages the researcher to work with the people being studied, involving them in formulating how they are spoken about in research and above all how they might benefit from the project.

This participation directly connects to the last values of *empowerment and understanding*. Qualitative research is concerned to make use of the research process as a way of empowering and supporting the participants in the research. The purpose is to value the understanding and the voices of the people and communities that are part of the research. This kind of empowerment is always intended to be part of the purpose of qualitative research.

## Getting Started

Before starting a small-scale empirical project, a series of important issues needs to be thought through. In the last part of this chapter I will set

10. Swinton and Mowat, *Practical Theology and Qualitative Research*, 13–15.

out some guidelines that you can follow as you begin to do a small-scale research project.

1. *Formulate a good research question that is open-ended but focused.* Practical theological research often starts with a particular issue or problem that needs further work. Solving a problem, however, will almost certainly be overambitious for a small-scale project. Most often the purpose of a project will be simply to understand a little more about something. It is worth adding that instrumental or pragmatic questions are not the best way to proceed. For example, a question like, "How can our youth ministry be more effective?" might be a felt and pressing need, but it is not a good research question for a qualitative inquiry. A better question might be, "How do our young people experience our youth ministry?" This is more open-ended. Of course, with the results from this kind of investigation, it would be possible to then formulate plans for how the youth ministry might be more effective. The point is that the research will open up a complex area of knowledge that can then be developed in more programmatic ways. The key to designing a project lies in formulating good research questions. A good research question will go to the heart of an issue, and it will open up inquiry rather than close it down. It is worth taking some time with the research question, writing it and rewriting it. It is common to have more than one research question, but when you are starting out it is best to try to be as focused as possible, so for a small-scale project I would recommend working with just one question.

2. *Keep the research question manageable in size and scope.* A research question needs to be related to a clear vision of what you are going to research. For example, you might start out with the idea that you want to research worship and young people. This is much too big for a small-scale project. To make this viable it needs to be more specific. This means that decisions need to be made about which young people you will actually research. You can narrow this down by saying that you want to research the young people in the youth group at Central Baptist Church. You might even narrow it down further to those who live in a particular area or have grown up in the church. So a research question might be something like, "How

do the young people who have grown up in the church engage with Sunday worship?" This is a manageable group, and there is a specific area designated for the research, but the question is exploratory in nature.

3. *Be realistic about the amount of material you are able to analyze.* However much experience we have in research, there is always a tendency for projects to be overambitious. One reason for this is that real life is complicated; everything connects with everything else. This means that developing a good research project will involve bracketing some things out and focusing on something that is achievable. When starting out as a researcher, it is common to underestimate how much material will be gathered and how overwhelming it can become. An interview that lasts an hour can run to more than ten transcribed pages. So a small number of interviews can generate so much text that it is quite a challenge to simply read through it all, let alone spend time immersed in what has been said to the extent that you can develop the kind of rich analysis that qualitative research requires. On the whole, especially when starting out, it is best to take the view that less is more.

4. *Identify your research method.* With a research question and a realistic and achievable intention, the next stage is to decide on the approach that will work best for the project. I have already introduced the key methods of observation, interviewing, working with texts, and recording and transcribing. Projects will often combine methods; it is a strategy to check findings. So if, for instance, the research has involved reading the minutes of church meetings to examine the mission strategy of the church over a period of time, semi-structured interviews could then be used to explore in more depth what has been discovered.

5. *Create a research plan.* The choice of research methods should be based on the research questions. When the methods have been decided, it is then necessary to draw up a research plan. This is just a simple statement of what you are going to do. Your plan should include what methods you will adopt and how large a sample or which group you will research.

6. *Do a practice run or pilot study.* It is often a good idea to pilot your study to see how your chosen method works. If it is doing interviews,

you can try out the questions and see how much data you generate. The purpose of a pilot is to fine-tune your research plan, so don't be afraid to make changes in light of what you find.

7. *Consider the ethical implications of the research.* This is particularly necessary when you conduct research that focuses on human subjects. If you are doing your research as part of a program of study, then your institution will have specific processes that you will need to go through for your project to receive ethical approval. The most important issue relates to people who might be considered high-risk. This would include children under sixteen, vulnerable adults, or offenders of any kind. My strong advice is that research with these groups should not be undertaken without the guidance of qualified supervisors in an academic setting where the project will be assessed by an institutional review board or research ethics committee. If you are an independent researcher and you do not plan to work with vulnerable people, then there are key guidelines that need to be followed:

a. Informed consent. You need to ensure that everyone taking part in the research understands what you are doing. This means giving them a sheet that explains the project and having them sign it, giving their consent to be a part of the project.

b. Anonymity. It is generally advisable to anonymize the data so the respondents cannot be identified. You need to make this clear on the consent form.

c. The right to withdraw. You need to make it clear that those taking part in the research can ask for their data to be removed from your research. You should give a specific date when this is no longer possible. This should also be set out on the consent form.

d. Data retention. You need to consider how long and in what way you will store the data and how you will ensure the privacy of your participants. This also needs to be explained on the consent form.

e. Sharing and privacy. You need to explain how you plan to use the data and in what contexts you will share it in the future. You must have the permission of every participant to use their data in teaching or at an academic conference, as well as in any written academic project you plan. This also needs to be set out on the consent form.

Research ethics is a complicated area, and there are specific issues around, for instance, video recordings or participant observation that need to be carefully thought through. There are a number of online resources that have been produced to help you think
through these issues. The Economic and Social Research Council
in the United Kingdom has a research ethics guidebook published
online that is a very useful resource.[11]

8. *Analyze your data.* Having gathered your data, transcribed your interviews, and made all of your notes from participation, then comes
the task of analysis. There are different ways of analyzing qualitative
data, but in a small-scale project the key idea is what is called coding. Coding is a way of organizing the data around broad themes.
This means reading through your notes several times and looking for
patterns that emerge. The process involves finding groups of related
material. When you are happy that these groups reflect what is in the
material, you can then go into more detail within each group. So, for
instance, in a set of interviews around the importance of community
in church, a key theme might be friendship. A more detailed analysis
might then look at the kinds of friendship being talked about. The
idea is to develop a detailed examination of the data.

9. *Share your conclusions with your research subjects.* When you have
analyzed the data, it is generally good practice to meet again with your
respondents to share your findings and to get their input on what you
are saying. This is valuable because it should help you to more fully
understand what you want to say. It is also important because it allows
the people you are researching to have an influence in the research
process. This kind of consulting, however, is always a negotiation, and
there may be things you feel are important to say that some people are
not entirely comfortable with. As a researcher, you need to balance
these kinds of reactions with your own role as a researcher.

10. *Present your data.* This is a particular skill. If you are writing up
your research, you need a balance between your own voice and the
voices of the people you are researching. It is vitally important that
you value and give enough space to the voices of the people you

11. "The Research Ethics Guidebook: A Resource for Social Scientists," http://www.ethics
guidebook.ac.uk.

have interviewed. It is good practice to include vivid and at times lengthy quotations from your material, but you will also need to re-present what you have found in your own words. It is best to be clear in your mind about what you have found in the data and what you want to add by way of interpretation of this material. It is hard to get this distinction when you are starting out, and one way to help with this is to separate out your interpretation from the presentation of the data. This could be in different chapters of a dissertation or in different sections of an essay.

11. *Pray.* Throughout the research process it is important to pray. Your research is not a secularized moment in your theological study. It is a way of paying attention and being present. Part of being present is to rest with your work in the presence of God.

# 10

# Producing Practical Theology

Practical theology has a purpose and a reason; it is meant to produce some-thing. It is mistaken to see the main product or result of practical theology as primarily an academic paper, a thesis, or even a book. Practical theology is not just a class taken as training for ministry; it is about changed lives. So the purpose and the eventual product of practical theology should be the transformation of individuals and communities. The transformation of individuals, society, and the church is a work of God that comes about through the work of the Holy Spirit. Practical theology, however, is a participation in this transforming work through the faithful pursuit of understanding that takes both theology and practice seriously. The end result of this activity is expression.

## Practical Theology and Expression

Expression takes many forms, but its purpose is to transform reflection into embodied faith. Expression, then, is both the act of being faithful to Christ and an attempt to communicate in society and in the Christian community what it means to be faithful. The kinds of expression that result from practical theology are many and various, so before discussing the different ways that practical theology might be written, this chapter will discuss forms of expression such as living, action, prayer, songs, and preaching.

## Living

The most fundamental product of practical theology will always be lives changed by the work of God. Living as a Christian involves a call to be a faithful follower of Christ, and the primary calling for the Christian is to share in the love of God. As the Gospel of John expresses it, "As the Father has loved me, so I have loved you; abide in my love. If you keep my commandments, you will abide in my love, just as I have kept my Father's commandments and abide in his love" (John 15:9–10). Love embraces family life, a missional engagement with society, and the fellowship of the Christian community. Such a calling is inevitably complex, with a whole host of possibilities and complicating factors that need to be understood and negotiated. This web of possibilities is the most basic arena out of which the call to be a faithful follower of Christ grows and is supported and encouraged by ordinary forms of practical theology that are part of the everyday practice of the church.

Being a faithful Christian in the world can be a kind of innate or intuitive practice. Living as a Christian will, however, entail times of reflection and adjustment. Elaine Graham, Heather Walton, and Frances Ward explore how practical theology can arise out of and contribute to the everyday lives and experiences of believers.[1] They speak about the life and experience of individual believers in much the same terms as we have seen used by Bonnie Miller-McLemore, as a kind of human document.[2] God is experienced in and through the inner life, and so through specific disciplines of reflection an awareness of a theology of the inner life and space can be developed. This leads to the possibility of what they call "theology by the heart."[3] This is a method of theological reflection that makes use of practices such as journal writing, personal letters, spiritual autobiography, and creative writing. The purpose behind these ways of doing practical theology is to enrich and develop a life of faith by taking time to pay attention to what it means to live as a Christian. This kind of personal reflection is actually

1. See Graham, Walton, and Ward, *Theological Reflection: Methods*. See also Graham, Walton, and Ward, *Theological Reflection: Sources*.
2. This is discussed more fully in chap. 3.
3. See Graham, Walton, and Ward, *Theological Reflection: Methods*, 18–45.

quite common. It is the sort of reflection that takes place in home groups or when individuals and groups go away for a retreat. These are everyday ways that practical theology already has a place in the life of the church, and the purpose of these kinds of expression is to help to renew the church.[4]

## Action

Often called praxis, this kind of practical theology emphasizes how God is active in history. Here theology is understood as the love of God in action. Action, rather than doctrinal formulation, is embraced as the locus for theological expression. Orthopraxy therefore takes priority over orthodoxy.[5] The notion of praxis has often been linked with theologies of liberation. Here action takes the form of education and the mobilization of collective forms of action that challenge and seek to change oppressive social, economic, and political structures.[6] The important contribution that this form of expression brings to practical theology is a constant reminder that thinking and action have a significant place within this field of theology.

There are different styles of learning and reflection. The most common type of practical theology is what might be called "theology on the move" or "theology on the go." This kind of reflection happens in the middle of practice and is therefore part of the action of ministry. The notion of pastoral imagination captures something of this. In chapter 5 we looked at Craig Dykstra's understanding of how ministers develop wisdom as they practice. Over time, this pastoral imagination develops and grows. Practitioners, however, need to be continually reviewing how they do the things that they do. Practitioners across a range of professions are continually engaged in evaluation and adjustment of their practice. This is a quite basic form of practical theology that operates in the context of action.

Practical theology that takes place as a continual reflection on action may not make reference to academic frameworks or sources, and it probably won't result in formal theological writing, although it is common in most areas of ministry and practice that people write reports and talk about their work in business papers and at meetings. These sorts of expression

4. Ibid., 2.
5. Ibid.
6. See Freire, *Pedagogy of the Oppressed*.

usually give an account of an activity, make some kind of assessment of what has been happening, and then out of this reflection develop strategies and plans for taking the work forward. In Christian organizations and churches, these ordinary kinds of reflection are intended to improve practice, but theological purposes and motivations are always present even if they are under the surface or implicit in how things are talked about. The more formal or academic forms of practical theology, given the prevalence of processes of reporting and reflecting in organizations, might be regarded as slightly more technical or intentional forms of a practice that take place on a regular basis in the context of doing ministry.

### Prayer

Prayer is one of the most important and profound forms of theological expression. I have already mentioned the quotation from Evagrius of Pontus that the theologian is one who prays truly, and the one who prays truly is a theologian. Prayer is traditionally very important in theology. My own church, the Church of England, has regarded the Book of Common Prayer, which reached its final form in 1662, as its most important theological document. As a result, saying the services in the book has always been regarded as a theology performed as prayer.

Prayers include the key elements that make up practical theology because they make a connection between life and God. An example of this is a simple prayer such as, "Lord, please bless Jane and John, who are expecting their first child." The prayer constructs a theological environment. This is one where the "Lord" is concerned with the two individuals and the birth of their child. The term "Lord" is not clarified in any way, so those sharing in the prayer can add their own understanding. This could be Christ, or it could be a more generic notion of God. As Lord, God/Christ is seen as active and capable of bringing about something called blessing. What this blessing is, however, is not explained. Blessing then becomes another shared theological concept that links those who are praying. Blessing is a blank space that allows for ambiguity about precisely what we are asking and also what we might be expecting. It might be understood as being specific to the individual who prays the prayer, such as a priest, or it might be seen as something that everyone shares in if the prayer happens during a church service.

The point is that a simple prayer generates a complex and multilayered practical theology in which the work of God, theological concepts, and life experience are interconnected. This connection between the life event of childbirth and the work of God/Christ made through the term "blessing" is a work of practical theology that takes place in the moments where the prayer is heard and then prayed.

Processing what is happening in the way I have set out here might be unusual, but the fact is, as Christians and as people who pray, we are able to operate this complex form of practical theology in a natural and intuitive way. Different prayers make connections in slightly different ways, and different people praying also make connections in different ways. This dynamic world of prayer is quite simply the heartland for practical theology. In the previous chapter, I gave an example of small-scale research into prayer. If you want to learn about your own lived theology, there is no better way than to spend a few moments thinking through how you pray, and you may find that exercise to be very helpful.

### Songs

Songs operate in much the same way as prayers. Songs create a theological world. In the world of the song, connections are made between life and God. Different songs do this in different ways, but what songs have in common is that they position the singer: they speak about the singer or congregation in such a way that we are somehow drawn into the world of the song as we sing. To take a well-known example, the song "Amazing Grace" works in just this way. The first verse is inscribed in many Christians' memories and spiritual lives.

> Amazing grace, how sweet the sound
> That saved a wretch like me.
> I once was lost but now am found,
> Was blind but now I see.

The story behind the song, written in 1779, locates these lyrics in the experience of the eighteenth-century British writer John Newton. Newton had been involved in the slave trade, but as a result of his experience of conversion, he eventually repented of his previous lifestyle and became a clergyman in the Church of England. Here, then, is a kind of practical theology that speaks of salvation not only in personal terms but also as a changed life that challenges accepted social structures.

From its origins, the song has been taken up and sung in almost every context imaginable. The link to slavery might continue to be a reference among those whose ancestors suffered that evil, but being lost and being made free might also take on a very different dynamic than the one Newton spoke about. For some, the lyric speaks of an experience of grace. Like the discussion of blessing, what grace might mean is left unexplained. It is, however, linked to salvation and to being lost and blind and the sense of being found and seeing. The experience of being a wretch might characterize being lost and blind, or it might be a sense of self that continues as the consciousness of being lost and blind is coterminous with the experience of salvation. The point is that "grace" has made the change. Of course, the rest of the lyric offers new and more complex insights.

The point I want to make here is that as we join in singing this song, we are invited to situate our own lives and experience in the dynamic of salvation. How we see our life and how we see salvation might be various, but the act of singing is an exercise in practical theology because it takes experience and theology seriously. I use the term "seriously" with deliberate intent because the song calls us to make connections between a gospel narrative and our own lives. We write ourselves into the song as we are singing. It is this personalized internal writing that is practical theology.

### Preaching

The act of preaching and the practice of listening to sermons are both forms of practical theology. Sermons make connections between experience and the Scriptures. Sometimes sermons are written first from experience and context, and then the connection to Scripture comes as part of developing a theological approach to life.[7] But very often a minister's preparation of a sermon begins with a passage from the Bible. This might be a passage that has been given to her, either because it is part of the sermon series or because it is the set passage in the lectionary, or it might be a passage she has selected. However it is done, the person who is planning the sermon has two main tasks at hand. The first is to understand and interpret the Bible as best as possible. The other task is, through

7. See chap. 6 under "Theological Reflection on the Self through Narration."

this process of seeking Christ in the Scriptures, to try to make a connection to the lives of the people who might listen to the sermon. This process of reading the Scriptures and trying to make connections to life is a vital form of practical theology that has been church practice since New Testament times.

Preaching is a performative form of practical theological expression. As performance, the focus is placed on the preacher, what she has composed, and how she delivers the sermon. The preacher, however, is only one half of what is taking place. The sermon has an audience. In fact, the intention behind the sermon is to "move" people through the act of preaching. Moving people is generally seen as a collaboration between the preacher and the work of the Holy Spirit. But those who listen are also active. As we listen, we engage in reflection and actively make links between our own lives and the ideas and stories presented in the sermon. This also is a way of doing practical theology because it takes the theology presented in the sermon, which itself might be a mix of experience, Scripture, and doctrine, and articulates these with life.

## Writing as Theological Reflection

This chapter has so far discussed the ways in which practical theology results in certain kinds of expression in the church and in the lives of individuals. I have included these perspectives because it balances out the assumption that the chief result of practical theology will be some kind of academic assignment. While this is important, it is also the case that writing lies at the heart of how we do practical theology. In her book *Writing Methods in Theological Reflection*, Heather Walton has explored the dynamics in writing as an approach to practical theology. The emphasis on writing, Walton argues, has the intention of fostering "a perception and awareness of God in the midst of life which will enable people of faith to orientate their practice according to their beliefs and values—and also to communicate their convictions in ways that are rooted in and relevant to the cultural context in which we live."[8] Practical theological writing needs to take place in a number of different genres, including sermons, liturgies, prayers, books, articles, essays, newspaper columns, radio scripts, and

8. Walton, *Writing Methods in Theological Reflection*, xi.

meditations. This is both a practical and a professional necessity. This writing is "performed" in a variety of different contexts, including churches, school halls, youth camps, and professional supervision.

The Bible is full of writing that reflects on experience. Walton cites Psalm 19 speaking about the stars and the glory of God, Psalm 46:1 in which God is a refuge, and Psalm 67 in which God dispenses justice. "The Bible is replete with narratives, dramas, and laments that shape religious reflection according to the conventions of particular genres and 'literary' traditions."[9] The Christian tradition is characterized by the use of experience in theological writing as part of the literature of devotion, including the testimonies of martyrs and visionaries; the narratives of pilgrims; texts of spiritual guidance; the imaginative work of, for instance, the Ignatian exercises; and the practices of personal testimony, confessional preaching, and self-examination.[10]

The range of different kinds of writing within practical theology is many and various, but it is likely that you will be expected to write an academic paper as part of your studies. The final section gives some practical advice for writing an academic paper based on the perspectives developed in this book.

## Writing an Academic Paper in Practical Theology

Different assignments will require different kinds of writing. A book review will be different from an observation of a worship event, and it will be different again from a paper that asks a question such as, what is practical theology? It is also important to take note of the expectations of the educational institutions and their formal ways of setting and assessing assignments. These differences mean that it is only possible to offer general advice for writing a paper in practical theology. Here are some things to keep in mind as you start to write. It might also be helpful to return to this after you have written your piece.

1. *Determine what kind of writing is expected.* The first consideration relates to the kind of writing that is expected. Sometimes practical

9. Ibid., xiii.
10. Ibid., xiii–xiv.

theology will ask for personal reflection and narrative, but if this is not the case, then the best advice is to write as if this were a paper in any other class. Use the same conventions of academic writing. This means paying attention to sources, discussing theories and ideas in detail, and critically evaluating the material that you are using. An academic paper will also need to have a system of referencing and a clear bibliography.

2. *Make a plan for answering the question being posed.* Academic writing at undergraduate and graduate levels normally involves a question. It seems obvious, but it is surprising how often students work hard on a paper, read many of the books and articles that are assigned, and then fail to address the question that has been set. Before writing, it is worth planning your paper in a way that makes clear how you answer the question, and then go back and check this frequently throughout your writing process.

3. *Locate your argument within a specific context.* I have argued that practical theology takes practice seriously. Taking practice seriously in academic writing means finding a way to offer a good account of what is actually happening in a lived situation. This might involve some kind of small-scale research project, but in a short paper it is more likely that the requirement will be to draw upon some empirical research that has already been written. Whichever is the case, it is important to firmly locate what is said in a context.

4. *Clarify what kind of theology is shaping the project.* In addition to paying attention to practice, a paper in practical theology should be theological. As has probably become clear in this book, theology is a complicated area. One way of tackling this step is to ask what kind of theology is shaping your project. Is it a theology that comes from the context and the practices of a community, or is it ideas and perspectives that come from the Bible or writers who might be outside the context? Being clear about what kind of theology you are working with is fundamental in practical theology.

5. *Determine where to situate the theological material.* If you are drawing on theology from writings and ideas that are outside your context, then a simple way to think about this is to ask the question, does this theological material come at the beginning or at the end of

the paper? If it is at the beginning, then usually this forms a way of framing the paper. The theology shapes the questions that are asked and perhaps poses a problem that you are setting out to solve. So you might discuss the biblical theology of grace and then look at practice to think about how grace is actually embodied. If the theology comes at the end, then it is usually used to offer a normative voice or perspective. Here in the practice, the focus might be on how a group or a community exercises a ministry of grace, and then this can be contrasted with or corrected by a biblical theology of grace.

6. *Draw on other academic disciplines beyond theology*. Most projects in practical theology are interdisciplinary. This means that, in addition to having a location in practice and context and paying attention to theology, there is usually an element that draws on another academic disciplinary area. Most common are papers that make use of the social sciences. These might include the psychology of religion, sociology, political theory, or anthropology. Drawing on the social sciences is one of the most common ways that practical theology takes practice and context seriously.

7. *Don't allow practical considerations to outweigh technical material*. Practical theology in all its forms always involves a discussion of how practice can be improved. This emphasis is most clear in Browning's understanding of practical theology as movement from practice to theory and then back to practice.[11] Many students are either active in practice as ministers or other kinds of Christian workers or are in training for these roles, so the practical consequences of the study are particularly important and significant. The temptation, then, is to spend most of the paper discussing the context and practical solutions, and as a result, the more technical theological or social scientific material is not covered adequately.

8. *Aim for balance among the various elements of the project*. From the point I have made above, it is clear that one of the central issues in any form of practical theology is the problem of balance—in other words, how the various elements in a project relate to one another and which elements ultimately have the most influence. This is not entirely straightforward, yet in many ways it is the crucial decision

11. Browning, *Fundamental Practical Theology*, 9.

that has to be made when doing practical theology. Practical theology has devised a variety of ways to deal with this complicated issue. The most common approach is to use a version of the pastoral cycle, which creates a sequence. At its most basic, it starts with practice.[12] Then it turns to the social sciences and other nontheological ways of exploring the context in more detail. The next stage involves theological reflection, and then finally it returns to offer ways to develop or improve practice. This is a very helpful way to practice doing practical theology. When using the cycle in a written project, the trick is to make sure that there is enough space given to each stage of the cycle and that none are missed.

9. *Be clear about your chosen method and how you have followed it*. If you are not using the pastoral cycle but have chosen another way to do practical theology, it is important to make this clear at the start of the paper and then show how you have followed your chosen method as you go through and eventually conclude the piece.

10. *Reflect prayerfully on the deeper purpose of the project*. Practical theology is not an end in itself. It is one way that Christians practice theology as "faith seeking understanding." This means that even when you are writing a paper for a class, the deeper purpose should not be lost. It is important to spend time reflecting on how your work might lead to transformation for yourself or other individuals, for society, and for the Christian community. This kind of attention I see as a form of prayer, because change comes from the work of the Spirit. So I would situate the practice-to-theory-to-practice model in prayer. My new model would look like this: prayer to theological reflection to prayer.

12. For more on the pastoral cycle see chap. 6.

# Bibliography

Ahern, Geoffrey, and Grace Davie. *Inner City God: The Nature of Belief in the Inner City*. London: Hodder and Stoughton, 1987.

Anderson, Ray S. *The Shape of Practical Theology: Empowering Ministry with Theological Praxis*. Downers Grove, IL: InterVarsity, 2001.

Anselm. *Anselm of Canterbury*. Vol. 1, *Monologion, Proslogion, Debate with Gaunilo, and Meditation on Human Redemption*. Translated and edited by Jasper Hopkins and Herbert Warren Richardson. Lewiston, NY: Edwin Mellen, 1974.

Archbishop's Council on Mission and Public Affairs. *Mission-Shaped Church*. New York: Seabury, 2004.

Arnold, Matthew. *Culture and Anarchy*. 1869. Reprint, Cambridge: Cambridge University Press, 1932.

Astley, Jeff. "The Analysis, Investigation and Application of Ordinary Theology," chap. 1 in Astley and Francis, *Exploring Ordinary Theology*.

———. *Ordinary Theology: Looking, Listening and Learning in Theology*. Aldershot: Ashgate, 2002.

Astley, Jeff, and Ann Christie. *Taking Ordinary Theology Seriously*. Cambridge: Grove Books, 2007.

Astley, Jeff, and Leslie J. Francis, eds. *Exploring Ordinary Theology: Everyday Christian Believing and the Church*. Aldershot: Ashgate, 2013.

Ballard, Paul, and John Pritchard. *Practical Theology in Action*. London: SPCK, 1996.

Bass, Dorothy C., and Craig Dykstra, eds. *For Life Abundant: Practical Theology, Theological Education, and Christian Ministry*. Grand Rapids: Eerdmans, 2008.

Bauman, Zygmunt. *Liquid Modernity*. Cambridge: Polity, 2000.

Beaudoin, Tom. *Virtual Faith: The Irreverent Spiritual Quest of Generation X*. New York: Jossey-Bass, 1998.

Beckford, Robert. *Jesus Is Dread: Black Theology and Black Culture in Britain*. London: Darton, Longman & Todd, 1998.

Berger, Peter. *The Social Reality of Religion*. London: Penguin, 1969.

Bevans, Stephen B. *Models of Contextual Theology*. 2nd ed. Maryknoll: Orbis, 2002.

Bosch, David J. *Transforming Mission: Paradigm Shifts in the Theology of Mission*. Maryknoll: Orbis, 1991.

Bradley, Ian. *Celtic Christianity: Making Myths and Chasing Dreams*. Edinburgh: Edinburgh University Press, 1999.

Browning, Don S. *A Fundamental Practical Theology: Descriptive and Strategic Proposals.* Minneapolis: Fortress, 1991.

Cabasilas, Nicholas. *Life in Christ.* Translated by Carmino J. De Catanzaro. Crestwood, NY: St. Vladimir's Seminary Press, 1975.

Cahalan, Kathleen, and James Nieman. "Mapping the Field of Practical Theology." In Bass and Dykstra, *Life Abundant*, 62–85.

Cameron, Helen, Deborah Bhatti, Catherine Duce, James Sweeney, and Clare Watkins. *Talking about God in Practice: Theological Action Research and Practical Theology.* London: SCM, 2010.

Cartledge, Mark J. *Testimony in the Spirit: Rescripting Ordinary Pentecostal Theology.* Aldershot: Ashgate, 2010.

Christie, Ann. *Ordinary Christology: Who Do You Say I Am? Answers from the Pews.* Aldershot: Ashgate, 2012.

Cobb, Kelton. *The Blackwell Guide to Theology and Popular Culture.* Malden, MA: Blackwell, 2005.

Cone, James. *The Spirituals and the Blues: An Interpretation.* New York: Seabury, 1972.

De Luna, Anita. *Faith Formation and Popular Religion: Lessons from the Tejano Experience.* Lanham, MD: Rowman & Littlefield, 2002.

Donovan, Vincent. *Christianity Rediscovered: An Epistle to the Masai.* London: SCM, 1978.

Dragas, George. *The Meaning of Theology: An Essay in Greek Patristics.* Darlington, 1980.

Duffy, Eamon. *The Stripping of the Altars: Traditional Religion in England, 1400–1580.* New Haven: Yale University Press, 1992.

Dykstra, Craig. "Pastoral and Ecclesial Imagination." In Bass and Dykstra, *Life Abundant*, 41–61.

Farley, Edward. *Theologia: The Fragmentation and Unity of Theological Education.* Philadelphia: Fortress, 1983.

Fennell, Catherine, ed. *The Anthropology of Christianity.* Durham, NC: Duke University Press, 2006.

Ford, David, ed. *The Modern Theologians: An Introduction to Christian Theology in the Twentieth Century.* Oxford: Wiley Blackwell, 2005.

Fowl, Stephen. *The Theological Interpretation of Scripture.* Eugene, OR: Cascade, 2009.

Fowler, James. *Stages of Faith: The Psychology of Human Development and the Quest for Meaning.* San Francisco: HarperSanFrancisco, 1981.

France, R. T., and Alister McGrath, eds. *Evangelical Anglicans: Their Role and Influence on the Church Today.* London: SPCK, 1993.

Freire, Paulo. *The Pedagogy of the Oppressed.* Harmondsworth, UK: Penguin, 1972.

Fulkerson, Mary McClintock. *Places of Redemption: Theology for a Worldly Church.* Oxford: Oxford University Press, 2007.

Gortner, David. *Varieties of Personal Theology: Charting the Beliefs and Values of American Young Adults.* Farnham: Ashgate, 2013.

Graham, Elaine. *Transforming Practice: Pastoral Theology in an Age of Uncertainty.* London: Mowbray, 1996.

Graham, Elaine, Heather Walton, and Frances Ward. *Theological Reflection: Methods.* London: SCM, 2005.

———. *Theological Reflection: Sources.* London: SCM, 2007.

Green, Laurie. *Let's Do Theology: Resources for Contextual Theology.* London: SCM, 1990.

Grenz, Stanley J., and John R. Franke. *Beyond Foundationalism: Shaping Theology in a Postmodern Context.* Louisville: Westminster John Knox, 2001.

Gutiérrez, Gustavo. *A Theology of Liberation.* Maryknoll: Orbis, 1973.

Hall, David D., ed. *Lived Religion in America: Toward a History of Practice.* Princeton: Princeton University Press, 1997.

Healy, Nicholas M. *Church, World and the Christian Life: Practical-Prophetic Ecclesiology.* Cambridge: Cambridge University Press, 2000.

Hegstad, Harald. *The Real Church: An Ecclesiology of the Visible*. Eugene, OR: Pickwick, 2013.

Heitink, Gerben. *Practical Theology: History, Theory, Action Domains*. Grand Rapids: Eerdmans, 1999.

Hervieu-Léger, Danièle. "'What Scripture Tells Me': Spontaneity and Regulation within the Catholic Charismatic Renewal." In Hall, *Lived Religion*, 22–40.

Hiltner, Seward. *Preface to Pastoral Theology*. Nashville: Abingdon, 1958.

Holmes, Stephen. "Three versus One? Some Problems of Social Trinitarianism." *Journal of Reformed Theology* 3 (2009): 77–89.

Jenks, Chris. *Culture*. 2nd ed. London: Routledge, 2005.

John XXIII. *Mater et Magistra* (Encyclical of Pope John XXIII on Christianity and Social Progress). May 15, 1961. http://w2.vatican.va/content/john-xxiii/en/encyclicals/documents/hf_j-xxiii_enc_15051961_mater.html.

Jolly, Karen Louise. *Popular Religion in Late Saxon England: Elf Charms in Context*. Chapel Hill: University of North Carolina Press, 1996.

Jones, Julie Scott, and Sal Watt, eds. *Ethnography in Social Science Practice*. Thousand Oaks, CA: Sage, 2010.

Kilby, Karen. "Is an Apophatic Trinitarianism Possible?" *International Journal of Systematic Theology* 12, no. 1 (January 2010): 65–77.

———. "Perichoresis and Projection: Problems with Social Doctrines of the Trinity." *New Blackfriars* 81, no. 957 (November 2000): 432–45.

Kolb, Daniel A. *Experiential Learning: Experience as a Source of Learning and Development*. Englewood Cliffs, NJ: Prentice Hall, 1984.

Kuhn, Thomas S. *The Structure of Scientific Revolutions*. Chicago: University of Chicago Press, 1962.

Küng, Hans, and David Tracy. *Paradigm Change in Theology: A Symposium for the Future*. Trans. Margaret Köhl. New York: Crossroad, 1989.

Kvale, Steinar. *InterViews: An Introduction to Qualitative Research Interviewing*. Thousand Oaks, CA: Sage, 1996.

Luhrmann, Tanya M. *When God Talks Back: Understanding the American Evangelical Relationship with God*. New York: Vintage Books, 2012.

Lynch, Gordon. *Understanding Theology and Popular Culture*. Oxford: Blackwell, 2005.

Maldonado, Louis. "Popular Religion: Its Dimensions, Levels and Types." *Concilium* 4, no. 186 (1986): 3–11.

Marsh, Charles. *God's Long Summer: Stories of Faith and Civil Rights*. Princeton: Princeton University Press, 1997.

Marsh, Charles, Peter Slade, and Sarah Azaransky, eds. *Lived Theology: New Perspectives on Method, Style, and Pedagogy*. Oxford: Oxford University Press, 2016.

McGann, Mary. *Exploring Music as Worship and Theology: Research in Liturgical Practice*. Collegeville: Liturgical, 2002.

———. *A Precious Fountain: Music in the Worship of an African American Catholic Community*. Collegeville: Liturgical, 2004.

McGuire, Meredith. *Lived Religion: Faith and Practice in Everyday Life*. Oxford: Oxford University Press, 2008.

Meeks, Wayne. *The First Urban Christians: The Social World of the Apostle Paul*. New Haven: Yale University Press, 1983.

Mette, Norbert. *Theorie der Praxis: Wissenschaftsgeschichtl. u. methodolog. Unters. zur Theorie-Praxis-Problematik innerhalb d. prakt. Theologie*. Dusseldorf: Patmos-Verlag, 1978.

Miller-McLemore, Bonnie. *Also a Mother: Work and Family as Theological Dilemma*. Nashville: Abingdon, 1994.

———. "Also a Pastoral Theologian: In Pursuit of Dynamic Theology (Or: Meditations from a Recalcitrant Heart)." *Pastoral Psychology* 59, no. 6 (2010): 813–28.

———. *Christian Theology in Practice: Discovering a Discipline*. Grand Rapids: Eerdmans, 2012.

———. "Feminism, Children, and Mothering: Three Books and Three Children Later." *Journal of Childhood and Religion* 2, no. 1 (January 2011), http://childhoodandreligion.com/wp-content/uploads/2015/03/Miller-McLemore-Jan-2011.pdf.

———. "Five Misunderstandings about Practical Theology." *International Journal of Practical Theology* 16, no. 1 (2012): 5–26.

———. *Let the Children Come: Reimagining Childhood from a Christian Perspective*. San Francisco: Jossey-Bass, 2003.

———. *The Wiley Blackwell Companion to Practical Theology*. Oxford: Blackwell, 2011.

Morgan, D. L. *Focus Groups as Qualitative Research*. 2nd ed. Thousand Oaks, CA: Sage, 1997.

Moschella, Mary Clark. *Ethnography as a Pastoral Practice: An Introduction*. Cleveland: Pilgrim, 2008.

Newbigin, Lesslie. *Foolishness to the Greeks: The Gospel and Western Culture*. Grand Rapids: Eerdmans, 1988.

———. *The Gospel in a Pluralist Society*. Grand Rapids: Eerdmans, 1989.

———. *The Other Side of 1984: Questions for the Churches*. Geneva: World Council of Churches, 1983.

Oden, Thomas C. *Care of Souls in the Classic Tradition*. Minneapolis: Fortress, 1984.

Ormerod, Neil. *Re-Visioning the Church: An Experiment in Systematic Historical Ecclesiology*. Minneapolis: Fortress, 2014.

Orsi, Robert. *Between Heaven and Earth: The Religious Worlds People Make and the Scholars Who Study Them*. Princeton: Princeton University Press, 2005.

———. "Everyday Miracles: The Study of Lived Religion." In Hall, *Lived Religion*, 3–21.

———. *The Madonna of 115th Street: Faith and Community in Italian Harlem, 1880–1950*. New Haven: Yale University Press, 1985.

Osmer, Richard. *Practical Theology: An Introduction*. Grand Rapids: Eerdmans, 2008.

Pattison, Stephen. *The Challenge of Practical Theology: Selected Essays*. London: Jessica Kingsley, 2007.

———. *A Critique of Pastoral Care*. 3rd ed. London: SCM, 2000.

Punch, K. F. *Survey Research: The Basics*. Thousand Oaks, CA: Sage, 2003.

Rogers, Andrew. *Congregational Hermeneutics: How Do We Read?* Aldershot: Ashgate, 2016.

Rogers, Clement. *An Introduction to the Study of Pastoral Theology*. Oxford: Clarendon, 1912.

Root, Andrew. *Christopraxis: A Practical Theology of the Cross*. Minneapolis: Fortress, 2014.

Sanneh, Lamin. *Translating the Message: The Missionary Impact on Culture*. Maryknoll: Orbis, 1991.

Scharen, Christian, ed. *Explorations in Ecclesiology and Ethnography*. Grand Rapids: Eerdmans, 2012.

———. *Fieldwork in Theology: Exploring the Social Context of God's Work in the World*. Grand Rapids: Baker Academic, 2015.

———. "Judicious Narratives: Ethnography as Ecclesiology." *Scottish Journal of Theology* 58, no. 2 (2005): 125–42.

———. *Public Worship and Public Work: Character and Commitment in Local Congregational Life*. Collegeville: Liturgical, 2004.

Scharen, Christian, and Aana Marie Vigen, eds. *Ethnography as Christian Theology and Ethics*. New York: Continuum, 2011.

Schön, Donald. *The Reflective Practitioner: How Professionals Think in Action*. New York: Basic Books, 1983.

Schreiter, Robert J. *Constructing Local Theologies*. Maryknoll: Orbis, 1985.

Shaw, Jane. *Octavia, Daughter of God: The Story of a Female Messiah and Her Followers*. New Haven: Yale University Press, 2011.

Silverman, David. *Interpreting Qualitative Data.* 3rd ed. Thousand Oaks, CA: Sage, 2006.

Storey, John. *Cultural Theory and Popular Culture: A Reader.* Englewood Cliffs, NJ: Prentice Hall, 1994.

Swinton, John, and Harriet Mowat. *Practical Theology and Qualitative Research.* London: SCM, 2006.

Tanner, Katherine. *Theories of Culture: A New Agenda for Theology.* Minneapolis: Augsburg Fortress, 1997.

Thompson, Judith. *Theological Reflection.* London: SCM, 2008.

Tillich, Paul. *Systematic Theology.* Vol. 1, *Reason and Revelation, Being and God.* Chicago: University of Chicago Press, 1951.

Torrance, T. F. *Reality and Evangelical Theology: The Realism of Christian Revelation.* Philadelphia: Westminster, 1982.

Tracy, David. *The Analogical Imagination: Christian Theology and the Culture of Pluralism.* New York: Continuum, 1981.

———. *Blessed Rage for Order: The New Pluralism in Theology.* Chicago: University of Chicago Press, 1975.

Treier, Daniel J. *Introducing Theological Interpretation of Scripture: Recovering a Christian Practice.* Grand Rapids: Baker Academic, 2008.

Tylor, Edward Burnett. *Primitive Culture: Researches into the Development of Mythology, Philosophy, Religion, Art, and Custom.* 1871. Reprint, Gloucester, MA: Smith, 1958.

van der Ven, Johannes A. *Practical Theology: An Empirical Approach.* Kampen: Kok Pharos, 1993.

Veling, Terry A. *Practical Theology: On Earth as It Is in Heaven.* Maryknoll: Orbis, 2005.

Village, Andrew. *The Bible and Lay People: An Empirical Approach to Ordinary Hermeneutics.* Aldershot: Ashgate, 2007.

Volf, Miroslav. *After Our Likeness: The Church as the Image of the Trinity.* Grand Rapids: Eerdmans, 1998.

Walton, Heather. "Calls to Preach." *Practical Theology* 2, no. 1 (2009): 63–74.

———. *Writing Methods in Theological Reflection.* London: SCM, 2014.

Ward, Pete. "Blueprint Ecclesiology and the Lived: Normativity as a Perilous Faithfulness." *Ecclesial Practices* 2, no. 1 (2015): 74–90.

———. *Growing Up Evangelical: Youthwork and the Making of a Subculture.* London: SPCK, 1996.

———, ed. *Perspectives on Ecclesiology and Ethnography.* Grand Rapids: Eerdmans, 2012.

Watkins, Clare. "Practical Ecclesiology: What Counts as Theology in Studying the Church?" With Helen Cameron, Deborah Bhatti, Catherine Duce, and James Sweeney. In Ward, *Perspectives on Ecclesiology and Ethnography,* 167–81.

Weston, Paul. *Lesslie Newbigin, Missionary Theologian: A Reader.* Grand Rapids: Eerdmans, 2006.

Williams, Raymond. *Culture.* London: Collins, 1981. Also published as *The Sociology of Culture.* New York: Schocken, 1982.

Williams, Rowan. *On Christian Theology.* Oxford: Blackwell, 2000.

Zizioulas, John. *Being as Communion.* Crestwood, NY: St. Vladimir's Seminary Press, 1985.

# Index

Made in the USA
Monee, IL
29 January 2021

59044675R00114